PHILLIES

Where Have You Gone?

FRAN ZIMNIUCH

WWW.SPORTSPUBLISHINGLLC.COM

Director of production: Susan M. Moyer
Book design: Jennifer Polson
Developmental editor: Scott Cimarusti
Project manager: Greg Hickman
Dust jacket design and imaging: Kenneth J. O'Brien
Card design: Christine Mohrbacher
Copy editor: Cynthia L. McNew
Cover photo: Mark Jones
Interior photos: Brace Photo, unless otherwise noted

ISBN: 1-58261-789-9

Printed in the United States.

*To my father, Eddie, who instilled the love of baseball
in me in August of 1963 when I saw my first and
only ballgame with him. To my mother, Catherine, who
encouraged my love of the game after he died.*

*For my sons, Brent and Kyle, who have learned to
enjoy the game by my side, who I hope will
continue to enjoy it long after I'm gone.*

*To Susan, for her love, understanding,
friendship, loyalty and encouragement.*

*For Lou Chimenti in thanks for more
than two decades of Journalism 101.*

*And to all of the Philadelphia Phillies players
who have made being a baseball fan such
an enjoyable experience throughout the years.*

CONTENTS

CHAPTER ONE: PITCHERS

Chapter Two: Infielders

Chapter Three: Outfielders

Chapter Four: Final Outs

ACKNOWLEDGMENTS

Phillies: Where Have You Gone? begins with Larry Andersen and ends with Lonnie Smith, as well as with a tribute to some former Phillies who have recently passed away. But it is these gentlemen and all the rest who played for the Phillies between 1950 and 1999 who deserve special recognition for their efforts on the baseball fields of that era, Connie Mack Stadium and Veterans Stadium. For a variety of reasons, a player sometimes stands out in your memory. That's why these players are remembered here. Some were stars; others hardly played at all, appearing in as little as one big-league game. But regardless of how successful they were, the effort was there and they deserve to be remembered.

I have no idea where or when this idea really began. But as the type of fan who used to enjoy listening to the announcers try to fill time during rain delays by interviewing players, I always liked learning about the players as people.

Did Dave Watkins really become a doctor, a goal during his lone big-league season? Why would a power-hitting first baseman like Costen Shockley retire at such a young age? Remember Fireball Freddie Wenz? After a successful stint with the Phillies, he never played again. And how did Richie Ashburn's old roomie, Ralph "Putsy" Caballero, get that unforgettable moniker? These are just some of the questions that are answered in *Phillies: Where Have You Gone?*

This project could never have happened were it not for some special people who aided me along the way. There is my old friend Dan Stephenson, better known as Video Dan, the Emmy Award winner from the Phillies organization, who thought my idea had merit and got me started. Then there was Tom Burgoyne, the close friend of the Phillie Phanatic and a fine author himself, who encouraged me to take the next step and helped me do so. I can't forget longtime Phillies announcer Chris Wheeler, who went out of his way to help me, and Phillies vice president, public relations, Larry Shenk.

Mike Pearson, Dean Reinke, Scott Rauguth and Scott Cimarusti from Sports Publishing L.L.C. nursed me along every step of the way and helped turn this idea into a reality.

Max Silberman and all of the wonderful people from the Philadelphia A's Historical Society helped me learn about some of the old-time Phillies. Joe Short, a former minor league baseball player whose best pitch was the Naked Fastball (you know, it had nothing on it) brought me up to date about later day players. And my favorite baseball writer, Bill Conlin, gave some useful tips as well.

And then there were the players, many of whom had not been interviewed about their careers in decades. They spent their precious time speaking about baseball and life, two things that have always gone hand in hand with me.

I thank all of the above.

PHILLIES
MANAGERS AND COACHES

THE FIFTIES
1950-1959

The Managers:

Eddie Sawyer	1948-52	(591 games, 296 wins-292 losses)
Steve O'Neill	1952-54	(324 games, 182 wins-140 losses)
Mayo Smith	1955-58	(545 games, 264 wins-281 losses)
Eddie Sawyer	1958-60	(227 games, 94 wins-132 losses)

The Coaches:

Benny Bengough (1946-58); Dick Carter (1959-60); Earle Combs (1954); Dusty Cooke (1948-52); George Earnshaw (1949-50); Tom Ferrick (1959); Eddie Mayo (1952-54); Maje McDonnell (1951, 54-57); Wally Moses (1954-58); Cy Perkins (1946-54); Bill Posedel (1958); Johnny Riddle (1959); Andy Seminick (1957-58); Whit Wyatt (1955-57).

THE SIXTIES
1960-1969

The Managers:

Andy Cohen	1960	(1 game, 1 win-no losses)
Gene Mauch	1960-68	(1331 games, 645 wins-684 losses)
George Myatt	1968	(2 games, 2 wins-no losses)
Bob Skinner	1968-69	(215 games, 92 wins-123 losses)
George Myatt	1969	(54 games, 19 wins-35 losses)

The Coaches:

Andy Cohen (1960); Billy DeMars (1969-81); Don Hoak (1967); Bob Lemon (1961); Harry "Peanuts" Lowrey (1960-66); Cal McLish (1965-66); George Myatt (1964-72); Bob Oldis (1964-66); Andy Seminick (1967-69); Larry Shepard (1967); Al Vincent (1961-63); Al Widmar (1962-64, 68-69).

THE SEVENTIES
1970-1979

The Managers:

Frank Lucchesi	1970-72	(399 games, 166-233)
Paul Owens	1972	(80 games, 33-47)
Danny Ozark	1973-79	(1,105 games, 594-510)
Dallas Green	1979-81	(299 games, 169-130)

The Coaches:

Carroll Beringer (1973-78); Brandy Davis (1972); Billy DeMars (1969-81); Doc Edwards (1970-72); Ray Rippelmeyer (1970-78); Harm Starrette (1979-81); Tony Taylor (1977-79); Bob Tiefenauer (1979); Bobby Wine (1972-83).

THE EIGHTIES
1980-1989

The Managers:

Dallas Green	1979-81	(299 games, 169-130)
Pat Corrales	1981-83	(248 games, 132-115)
Paul Owens	1983-84	(239 games, 128-111)
John Felske	1985-87	(384 games, 190-194)
Lee Elia	1987-88	(254 games, 111-142)
John Vukovich	1988	(9 games, 5-4)
Nick Leyva	1989-91	(338 games, 148-189)

The Coaches:

Ruben Amaro (1980-81); Larry Bowa (1988-96); Dave Bristol (1982-85 & 88); Jim Davenport (1986-87); Billy DeMars (1969-81); Lee Elia (1980-81 & 85-87); John Felske (1984); Deron Johnson (1982-84); Darold Knowles (1989-90); Denis Menke (1989-96); Claude Osteen (1982-88); Mike Ryan (1980-95); Herm Starrette (1979-81); Tony Taylor (1988-89); Del Unser (1985-88); John Vukovich (1988-present); Bobby Wine (1972-83).

THE NINETIES
1990-1999

The Managers:

Nick Leyva	1989-91	(338 games, 148 wins-189 losses)
Jim Fregosi	1991-96	(894 games, 431 wins-463 losses)
Terry Francona	1997-00	(648 games, 285 wins-363 losses)

The Coaches:

Larry Bowa (1988-96); Dave Cash (1996); Galen Cisco (1997-00); Chuck Cottier (1997-00); Ramon Henderson (1998-present); Darold Knowles (1989-90); Hal Lanier (1990-91); Hal McRae (1997-00); Brad Mills (1997-00); Johnny Podres (1991-96); Joe Rigoli (1996-97); Mel Roberts (1992-95); Mike Ryan (1980-95); John Vukovich (1988-present); Jim Wright (1996).

Chapter 1

PITCHERS

LARRY ANDERSEN

L arry Andersen pitched in 699 career big-league games, all but one as a reliever. His one start came with the Mariners in 1982. Pitching out of the bullpen, this workhorse with a sometimes unhittable slider pitched in at least 30 games 12 times during his career. Primarily used as a setup man, he did save 13 games for the '91 Padres. Andy was a member of the '83 and '93 Phillies World Series teams.

After three brief look-sees with the Cleveland Indians, Anderson finally got an opportunity to pitch regularly with the Seattle Mariners, going 3-3 in 1981 in 41 games. He also appeared in 40 games the following season before being purchased by the Phillies in 1983. He went 1-0 in 17 games with an ERA of 2.39 and also pitched well in two World Series appearances against the Baltimore Orioles in a losing cause.

After working in 64 and 57 games over the next two seasons, Andy spent the next five seasons in Houston. He went 9-5 in 1987 in 67 games with a 3.45 ERA. After pitching in at least 50 games over the next three years, he was dealt to the Boston Red Sox for Jeff Bagwell, who went on to become one of the finest players in Astros history.

PHILLIES

LARRY ANDERSEN

#47 LARRY ANDERSEN • PITCHER

Phillies, Indians, Mariners, Astros, Red Sox, Padres

Born: 5/6/1953 Portland OR
Height: 6-3 • Weight: 205 lbs. • Bats right • Throws right
17 year Major League Career: 40-39
Phillies 6 years • Major League Debut: 1975

Andersen appeared in just 15 games for Boston and was 0-1 in three games in the ALCS.

He then signed as a free agent with the San Diego Padres and responded with a 4-5 record over a two-year period with 15 saves in 72 total games before returning to the Phillies for the 1993 and '94 seasons.

In the Phillies' World Series season of '93, Andersen appeared in 64 games with a 3-2 record and an ERA of 2.92. His slider worked to perfection most of that season against right-handed hitters.

Also well known as one of baseball's worst-hitting pitchers, he had just five hits in 38 career at-bats for a meek .132 average.

Larry Andersen is also known as one of the great jokesters of the game. Just some of his favorite axioms about baseball and life include, "Why do you park in the driveway?" "Why do people sing, 'Take Me Out to the Ballgame' when they're already there?" and "If he's a good fastball hitter, should I throw him a bad fastball?"

After his playing career ended, he served as a minor league pitching instructor for the organization, helping young pitchers hone their skills.

Following the untimely death of Philadelphia icon player and announcer Richie Ashburn, Andersen became a Phillies broadcaster. His goofy and off-beat but well appreciated sense of humor has served him well in the booth. Not to mention his astute knowledge of the game.

JACK BRITTIN

This right-hander was 0-0 in just six relief appearances with the Phillies in 1950 and 1951. Considered a top prospect in the Phillies organization, Jack Brittin had health problems that affected his pitching. He went 7-11 for the 1950 Toronto Maple Leafs but spent nearly two months of the season with leg numbness. A true fighter, Brittin pitched well enough to be recalled by the Phillies late in the season.

He was eventually released by the team in the spring of 1952. Never a quitter, Brittin went on to become a top hurler with the Atlanta Crackers of the Southern Association and for Huron of the Basin League. But the continued arm and leg problems plagued him and eventually caused his retirement from the game in 1954.

It was not until 1956 that Jack Brittin was diagnosed with multiple sclerosis. He fought the disease and became a teacher who taught physical education and coached in Springfield, Illinois. The disease continued to interfere with his life, and he was forced to quit in 1958 due to ill health.

Once again, Brittin bounced back and became employed by the Office of Public Instruction of the Illinois State Board of Educa-

jack brittin

PHILLIES   PITCHER

#41 JACK BRITTIN • PITCHER
Phillies

Born: 3/4/1924 Athens IL • Died: 1/5/94 Springfield IL
Height: 5-11 • Weight: 175 lbs. • Bats right • Throws right
2 year Major League Career: 0-0
Phillies 2 years • Major League Debut: 1950

tion. He married a childhood classmate and later worked for the Teachers Retirement System and the State Board of Education until his retirement in 1989.

He died of a heart attack brought on by his MS in 1994.

JACK BALDSCHUN

J ack Baldschun was one of the first pitchers, along with Ruben Gomez, to utilize the screwball on a regular basis. Following his minor league career that included stops in towns like Thibodeau, Wausau, Savannah, Albuquerque, Visalia and Topeka, Baldschun made his way to the Show.

In the early '60s, he was the bellwether of the Phillies bullpen. He won 12 games for the '62 Phils and 11 in '63. He also saved 59 games for the club over a five-year period, including 21 for the ill-fated 1964 team.

"The Phillies organization was really good to me," he said. "We were on good terms. Gene Mauch and I got along really well. I picked up the screwball from working with a catcher named Dick Kennedy. I had good control of the pitch and could throw it for strikes."

As a key member of the '64 team, Baldschun was part of the early-season ecstasy, which ended in agony for the entire city. Mauch took some criticism for using top starters Jim Bunning and Chris Short with little rest in between starts, even though Dennis Bennett, Ray Culp and a young Rick Wise were also available.

"In 1964 it got to the point where I thought Gene was trying his best," he said. "He tried to win it with Bunning and Short early to

Photo provided by author

#27 JACK BALDSCHUN • PITCHER

Phillies, Reds, Padres

Born: 10/16/1936 Greenville OH
Height: 6-0 • Weight: 190 lbs. • Bats right • Throws right
9 year Major League Career: 48-41 • 60 saves
Phillies 5 years • Major League Debut: 1961

give everybody else a rest. Each night we tried the best we could, but we ended up out of it. I don't really blame Gene that much for using Bunning and Short that way."

After his time in Philadelphia, Baldschun pitched for Cincinnati in 1966 and '67 with a 1-5 mark. He resurfaced in San Diego with the Padres in 1969 with a 7-2 record. His big-league career ended the following season after just 12 appearances.

Jack Baldschun has nothing but fond memories of his five years in Philadelphia.

"I had a fantastic time there," he said. "The wife and I always thought that we might end up living there, but we had family considerations and moved back to Green Bay. We play a lot of golf and travel a lot now."

Baldschun was drafted by the Phillies from the Minnesota Twins on November 28, 1960 in the Rule V draft. On December 6, 1965, he was traded to the Baltimore Orioles in exchange for Jackie Brandt and Darold Knowles.

Following baseball he started a contracting business with his brother-in-law and then worked for a lumber supply company for 25 years before retiring in the late '90s.

But even though the '64 Phillies didn't win the pennant in that star-crossed season, Jack Baldschun was one of the players who gave it his all and helped get them in a position to win.

"At the end of the day I guess the good Lord just didn't want us to win it," he said.

BO
BELINSKY

Robert Bo Belinsky could pitch, but his reputation was as one of the great playboys of the western world. In the early '60s, he managed to take a regular turn in the Los Angeles Angels' starting rotation with his partner in fun, Dean Chance, while being romantically linked to the likes of Ann-Margaret, Connie Stevens, Tina Louise and Mamie Van Doren.

When Bo settled down and got married, it was to Jo Collins, who just happened to be the 1965 Playboy Playmate of the Year. Belinsky was 10-11 in his rookie campaign with the Angels in 1962 and hurled a no-hitter against the Baltimore Orioles, only adding to his mystique.

In fairness to this southpaw, baseball success was not an overnight happening, as he toiled for six minor league seasons before getting his chance with the Angels. He went 13-6 for Pensacola in 1957 and won 10 games for Aberdeen the following year.

After paying his dues in the minor leagues, he made quite an impression in his rookie year. He followed up with a 2-9 1963 season, but rebounded nicely, going 9-8 in '64 before being traded to the Phillies.

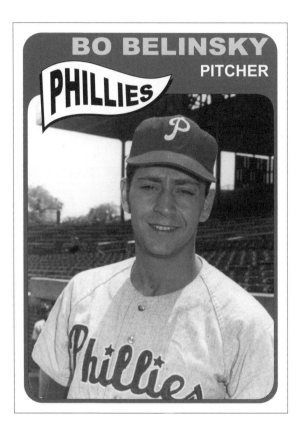

#33 BO BELINSKY • PITCHER
Phillies, Angels, Reds, Astros, Pirates

Born: 12/7/1936 New York NY • Died: 11/23/2001 Las Vegas NV
Height: 6-2 • Weight: 191 lbs. • Bats left • Throws left
8 year Major League Career: 28-51
Phillies 2 years • Major League Debut: 1962

Over the next five seasons, the best Belinsky could muster was four wins for the '65 Phillies and three wins for the Astros in 1967. He closed out his big-league career in 1970 appearing in three games with the Reds.

Bo also made guest appearances on various television shows and a few movies. He penned a book called, *Pitching and Wooing*, in which he described more of the wooing aspects of his life than his pitching exploits.

On the field, Bo Belinsky was never able to match his rookie numbers and bounced around from team to team.

Even though he won just 28 games in his major league career, Bo Belinsky was the premier baseball playboy in the 1960s.

Belinsky was traded to the Phillies from the California Angels on December 3, 1964 in exchange for Rudy May and Costen Shockley. He was drafted by the Houston Astros from the Phillies on November 28, 1966 in the Rule V draft.

In later years, he became a drug and alcohol abuse counselor. He passed away of a heart attack in Las Vegas.

JIM BUNNING

This right-hander with a sweeping sidearm delivery was an intimidating hurler for much of his career. He put everything into each pitch, finishing his delivery with his glove hand actually touching the ground to the side of the mound to keep him from falling. Known as an incredible competitor, he won 224 games en route to his Hall of Fame induction. Bunning showed consistency, winning 20 games just once in 1957 for Detroit with 19 victories four times and 17 on three different occasions. In fact, while pitching for the Phillies in 1967, he won 17 games, but set a major league record by losing five 1-0 games.

Bunning was the first pitcher since Cy Young to win over 100 games in each league and to strike out over 1,000 in each league. When he retired from the game, only Walter Johnson had more than his 2,885 strikeouts. He also pitched no-hitters in both leagues including his Phillies gem in 1964, a perfect game on Father's Day against the New York Mets. That marked the first National League perfect game since 1880.

"He should have been in the Hall of Fame sooner," said Ray Culp, former Phillies pitcher. "He was my roomie for two years. Jim

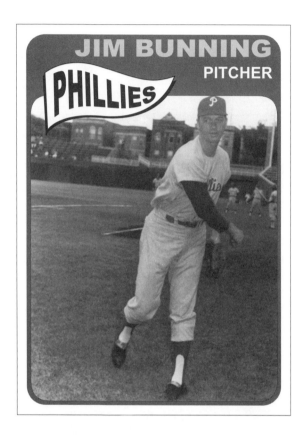

#14 JIM BUNNING • PITCHER
Phillies, Tigers, Pirates, Dodgers

Born: 10/23/1931 Southgate KY
Height: 6-3 • Weight: 195 lbs. • Bats right • Throws right
17 year Major League Career: 224-184
Phillies 6 years • Major League Debut: 1955

is a highly intelligent guy and a great family man. And he was a great pitcher. He was as good a pitcher as I ever played with."

Whether he was on the mound or not, Jim Bunning has always dominated his surroundings. One of the best pitchers of his era, he was also one of the founders of the players union and he helped establish the players' pension plan.

"Jim was a very serious, no-nonsense player," said outfielder Doug Clemens. "He was bright, sharp and intelligent and he never gave in to anybody. He loved competition. When I became a teammate, we played bridge together all the time. I got to know Jim well."

He was also a player and person who was always interested in helping young players. Even a pitcher from a newer generation.

"I'll never forget something that Jim Bunning told me," said Larry Christenson, who pitched for the Phillies in the '70s and '80s. "He said, 'Young man, if you get 40 starts a year, 10 will be fabulous, 10 will be awful and the other 20 will make you a pitcher.'"

Bunning was traded by the Detroit Tigers with Gus Triandos on December 4, 1963, to the Phillies in exchange for Don Demeter and Jack Hamilton. On December 15, 1967, the Phillies traded him to the Pittsburgh Pirates for Don Money, Woodie Fryman, Bill Laxton and Harold Clem. He signed as a free agent with the Phillies on October 29, 1969.

Following his outstanding career, Bunning later managed in the Phillies' minor league system for five years before becoming a player agent. He then got involved in politics and was elected to the Kentucky state legislature. After an unsuccessful run for governor, he was elected to the U.S. House of Representatives in 1986 as a Republican from a heavily Democratic district. His hard work and involvement in economic issues quickly won him the respect of his colleagues and a seat on the influential Ways and Means Committee, making him the first Kentucky representative in 20 years and the first Republican Kentuckian to serve on the powerful committee in the century.

Then in 1998, following a hard-fought campaign, Bunning was elected to the U.S. Senate. He served on the Finance Committee during the 108th Congress and has also been a member of the Committee on Banking, Housing and Urban Affairs.

He and his wife Mary have nine children and 35 grandchildren.

STEVE CARLTON

When the Phillies acquired this big left-hander in February of 1972, the move was not a popular one among the fans. Staff ace Rick Wise was dealt to the Cardinals to get Carlton. Both pitchers were involved in contract disputes, which was the primary reason for the deal. But Lefty soon won over all of the critics by winning 27 games in 1972.

"I'll never forget the year that Steve had in 1972," said former teammate Tommy Hutton. "He won 27 games on a team that was not very good. I think that was the best year a pitcher ever had."

The tall left-hander enjoyed success with the Cardinals, winning 74 games over a five-year span, including 20 for the 1971 Cards. But his breakout season with the Phillies made him a folk hero, winning 27 games for a club that only won a total of 57 times. He led the league in wins and ERA, with a stunning 1.97 mark. That season also saw Carlton enjoy a 15-game winning streak and become the second lefty to reach to 300-strikeout level.

He was a six-time 20-game winner, a four-time Cy Young winner and the most dominating pitcher of his era. The best slider in the game helped Lefty be the dominant pitcher that he was. But his self-confidence and positive attitude were every bit as dominant.

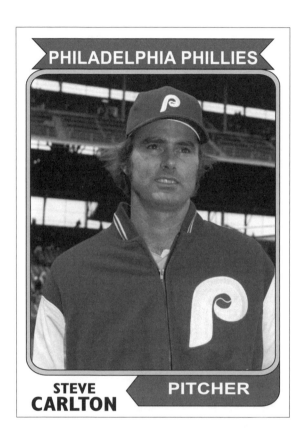

PHILADELPHIA PHILLIES

STEVE
CARLTON

PITCHER

#32 STEVE CARLTON • PITCHER
Phillies, Cards, Twins, Giants, White Sox, Indians

Born: 12/22/1944 Miami FL
Height: 6-4 • Weight: 210 lbs. • Bats left • Throws left
24 year Major League Career: 329-244
Phillies 15 years • Major League Debut: 1965

"I learned so much about the game from Steve Carlton," said another former teammate, pitcher Jim Lonborg. "He taught me about attitude and the right frame of mind. Don't pitch like you're afraid to lose. Pitch with the confidence that you're going to win."

Although he stopped talking to the press in 1978, saying that "Policy is policy," Carlton remained a popular player in the locker room and with the fans.

"You couldn't ask for a better teammate than Lefty," said former Phillies reliever Gene Garber. "It was an honor and a privilege to play on the same team as Lefty. I really liked him as a person; he was great to me. When you get an opportunity to play with one of the greatest players in the history of the game, it's a lot of fun."

Carlton won 20 games in '76, 23 in '77, 24 in '80 and 23 in 1982. This workhorse threw more than 300 innings twice and over 200 innings 16 times during his big-league career.

An intense competitor who prided himself on his physical conditioning, Carlton went through up to two hours a day of hard workouts with Phillies conditioning coach Gus Hoefling.

His last big year in the major leagues was 1984 when he went 13-7 for the Phils at the age of 39. A 1-8 injury-plagued season followed in 1985, and Lefty's Philadelphia career ended with a 4-8 mark in 1986.

Confident that he could still pitch, he then had stops with the Giants, White Sox, Indians and Twins. But over the last three years of his career, Carlton was just 11-17.

He now enjoys his retirement, talks to the press occasionally and travels to help Major League Baseball and the Hall of Fame, where he is a proud member.

DON CARMAN

Don Carman was one of those pitchers who had the ability to either start or relieve. While that gives a manager some flexibility, it can often be difficult for a pitcher to feel at home in either role.

Carman broke in to the big leagues with two brief tryouts with the team in 1983 and 1984. He made the Show for good in '85 and responded with a 9-4 record out of the bullpen, saving seven games in 71 appearances.

Impressed with his strong arm and great stuff, the Phillies converted Carman into a starter during the 1986 season, and he responded with a 10-5 record. His best major league season came in the following year when he posted a 13-11 record in 35 games as a starter. He did, however, surrender 34 home runs and had an ERA over 4.00. After going 10-14 in 1988 and 5-15 in '89, Carman once again became a reliever. He went back to the bullpen, pitching effectively in 59 games for the '90 Phils, going 6-2.

He became a free agent that winter and signed with Houston before pitching briefly for the Reds and Rangers, where he finished up in '92.

"I loved my time with the Phillies," Carman said.

DON CARMAN

#39 DON CARMAN • PITCHER

Phillies, Reds, Rangers

Born: 8/14/1959 Oklahoma City OK
Height: 6-3 • Weight: 195 lbs. • Bats left • Throws left
10 year Major League Career: 53-54
Phillies 8 years • Major League Debut: 1983

"I felt like it was my home, and you develop a relationship with the area and its fans. The city itself could be intimidating. I was from a town of 150 people in Oklahoma. The first time I drove into Philly, I got lost. But the town could also be inspiring."

With the experience of playing in Philadelphia as well as the education to analyze it, Carman spoke about the tough image that the City of Brotherly Love endures.

"I think the people in the city like the tough-guy rap," he said. "The city likes the tough image. The feeling I got was that you have to be tough to come to Philly."

Tough or not, the fans accepted Don Carman as a favorite all through his time with the Phillies. He had a rewarding relationship with the fans and the city.

"I hope they remember me as a friend who was on the team," he said. "I was a friend and a player who always tried to involve the fans."

Always known for his sense of humor, he once posted a list of 37 responses to questions he expected reporters to ask him on his locker.

Now a resident of Naples, Florida, Don Carman works with the pitching staff at Naples High School (the Golden Eagles) as well as Little League teams. After his career ended, he went back to school earned a degree in sports psychology at Florida Gulf Coast University in 1997. He now works with his former agent, Scott Boras, as a sports psychologist.

Carman meets with some of the players whom Boras represents and helps them get through bad stretches on and off the field and maintain a good mental approach to the game.

"I try to work with the players about any problems they might have personally or with their relationships," Carman said. "Mostly I'm dealing with coping skills with life and working with them on their approach to the game itself. It was always my intent to get into this field."

LARRY CHRISTENSON

L.C. played his entire career with the Phillies after being drafted in the first round of the 1972 amateur draft, the third pick overall. He first appeared with the club in 1972 and went 1-4 in 10 games. At the age of 19, Larry Christenson was the youngest player in the major leagues. He realized early on that the Phillies organization was something special.

"I remember when I first signed in front of Bob Carpenter," Christenson said. "He was so friendly and supportive. So was his entire family and Ruly Carpenter and his family. Then there was Paul Owens, Danny Ozark, Dallas Green, Bill Giles, Dave Montgomery and others. They were some really special family and friends. Those days, everyone wanted to play in Philly.

"Ruly liked to pull up a chair and talk baseball before and after the games. He was a great friend. We had a collection of great players, and I had some great teammates."

Sent to Toledo of the Pacific Coast League in 1974 for some additional experience, Christenson responded with an 11-9 season prior to another 10-game stint with the Phillies, going 1-1.

He made it to the Show for good in 1975 with an 11-6 season and a 3.66 ERA. Christenson then sandwiched a pair of 13-victory

Photo © The Phillies

PHILADELPHIA PHILLIES

LARRY
CHRISTENSON
PITCHER

#38 LARRY CHRISTENSON • PITCHER

Phillies

Born: 11/10/1953 Everett WA
Height: 6-4 • Weight: 215 lbs. • Bats right • Throws right
11 Year Major League Career: 83-71
Phillies 11 years • Major League Debut: 1973

campaigns around his best big-league season, 1977, when he went 19-6. Also known as a fine hitter, Christenson hit 11 home runs during his career, including three in 1977.

He was a fine young pitcher who was part of the world championship team in 1980. But with his father seriously ill in the hospital, Christenson had a horrible outing against the Kansas City Royals in the Fall Classic. It is a wound that still hurts even all these years later.

"It was a terrible experience," he said.

"It happened so fast. I just wish I could turn the clock back. I was a part of the team that year. But my father was in a coma and it was such an important game. That game still haunts me. It has always haunted me."

Arm miseries began to plague him, and the big right-hander never won more than nine games in a season after that. Finally, early in the 1983 season, his elbow simply gave out after nine starts.

"My elbow kind of blew up," he said.

"I went searching around the country talking to doctors and wound up having my fourth and fifth operations. I had 25 bone spurs and chips taken out. I did try to make a comeback, but my arm didn't respond well. I was no longer able to play."

So the young man reached the end at age 29 and gave up hopes of a comeback by the time he was 31. Not really interested in staying in the game as a coach, he began to transition to a new life after baseball.

"I was never a big fan of the game," he said.

"I could pitch and play the game and I pitched through pain and injury. But I saw the politics involved. I give coaches a lot of credit. They are dedicated baseball people. I moved on. I was proud of my career, but I turned the page a long time ago."

Since being forced from the game, Christenson has been involved in the investment business for the past 19 years and currently sells institutional investment services. The single-minded determination that enabled him to be successful as a pitcher has only intensified in his business career.

"I wanted to get involved with something and I stayed with it and did not falter," he said. "The biggest mistake that former athletes make is that they don't stick with something. I believe in honesty, integrity and trust. That's my mission statement. Building relationships is a key element in business and life."

Still one of the good guys of the game, Larry Christenson has maintained his baseball and business relationships and is active in the community and with numerous charities. As a player who has thrived in life since his baseball career ended, he still has the heart of an athlete who loved what he did.

"I still to this day have dreams where I'm in a uniform, getting ready to pitch," he said. "Then I wake up. I'm glad I played my entire career in Philadelphia. You couldn't find a better organization. I enjoyed my career and was fortunate enough to play as long as I did and I played with a lot of pain. But I was young enough to do something else."

Where Have You Gone?

LARRY COLTON

arry Colton has had two driving elements in his life: athletics early on, followed by teaching and writing after his baseball career ended. But even as a minor league pitcher, this University of California at Berkeley grad was not your typical jock. One season, a Phillies minor league coach named Moose Johnson kept calling him "Red." Colton, who does not have red hair, finally asked the coach about his new found nickname. With a southern drawl, Johnson replied, " 'Cause you're one of them guys that has read a book."

Not only has Larry "Read" Colton read books, but following his baseball career, he has become a highly acclaimed author of books such as *Goat Brothers*, the story of five University of California at Berkeley frat brothers and their lives since the 1960s. Colton also was nominated for a Pulitzer Prize in Literature in 2000 for the highly regarded *Counting Coup: A True Story of Basketball and Honor on the Little Big Horn*.

While he would surely like to have pitched in more than just one major league game, the premature end to Larry Colton's baseball career led him to teaching and writing. As is often said, when one door closes, a window sometimes opens.

Photo provided by Larry Colton

#21 LARRY COLTON • PITCHER
Phillies

Born: 6/8/1942 Los Angeles CA
Height: 6-3 • Weight: 200 lbs. • Bats left • Throws left
1 year Major League Career: 0-0
Phillies 1 year • Major League Debut: 1968

"I never got to really find out whether I could have done any-thing in the big leagues," Colton said. "People say what a shame that was, but it was really fate. If my career would have gone on as I had hoped, I probably would have become a Sam Malone, the bar owner in *Cheers*. But my life was redirected and I became a writer, which really defines me now."

Colton was a highly regarded prospect in the Phillies organiza-tion, winning 14 games at their Triple A affiliate in San Diego in 1967 with an ERA under 3.00. He made the Phillies' opening day roster in 1968 and pitched two innings against the Cincinnati Reds in his debut, giving up one run in two innings and getting two strikeouts. But on the same evening that Senator Robert F. Kennedy was shot, Larry Colton's life changed.

During a West Coast road trip with the Phillies, he was out catching up with an old friend at a California pub called The Jolly Friar. After his friend had words with some patrons of the establish-ment, the two were jumped as they left the place. Later that night, Colton, who fell hard on his left shoulder during the altercation, reached to pick up the phone in his hotel room, separating the shoul-der as a result of the tussle. He missed most of that season and came back to pitch effectively again at the minor league level. But it was never quite the same.

"I won 11 or 12 games the following year, but I wasn't as good," Colton said. "Something was missing. With all that was going on in the world and Vietnam, I just had trouble focusing."

He became the player to be named later in a trade that sent him and Johnny Callison to the Chicago Cubs in exchange for pitcher Dick Selma and outfielder Oscar Gamble.

After another successful Triple A season in the Cubs organiza-tion, Colton retired and became a teacher. But the latent writer in him began to appear, and he soon had articles published in periodi-cals such as *Esquire*, *Sports Illustrated* and the *New York Times*. The guy who had been best known during his baseball career for being the former son-in-law of actress Heddy Lamar soon became a best-selling author. While his baseball career was cut short, his writing career has taken him to new heights.

"I did achieve my dream of being a big-league ball player, but it was unfulfilled," he said. "My life has put me in two different worlds, athletics and literature. Baseball defined who I was for 26 years. Now in my literary career, I sometimes still think of myself as an impostor. I still don't believe the success I've had at times. All of my focus growing up was baseball. I learned to write by writing, I never took any journalism courses or writing courses. I starting selling articles while I was still teaching. But once I got that thing in me, I just had to write. I struggled at first, trying to raise a family, but I've done it now for 25 years.

"My transition to writing was sort of like jumping over the cliff. I just believed I could do it and didn't want to wonder if I could have 30 years down the line."

Just who is Larry Colton, the pitcher or the writer?

"I'm the writer now," he said. "I've been that other person too, but it doesn't seem like me now. I guess I'd like to be thought of as both, with a special emphasis on the writing. I'm proud of both careers but most proud of being a writer."

Much like Archibald "Moonlight" Graham, the ballplayer-turned-doctor in the movie *Field of Dreams*, Larry Colton only got to play in one major league game. But from his perspective and from that of his many literary fans, the real tragedy would have been if he were a writer for just one day.

RAY CULP

R ay Culp broke in with a splash in 1963, earning NL Rookie Pitcher of the Year honors as well as making the All-Star Game with his 14-11 record. The young right-hander had a disappointing '64 campaign, but rebounded with another 14-win season in 1965. Even early in his career, Culp had shoulder problems that would require major surgery in the 1970s.

"The Phillies signed me at age 17 in 1959, and they were the team I got to the big leagues with," Culp said. "I really enjoyed it. When I first went there I wasn't very old. What probably helped my career the most was being a teammate of Roger Craig, who taught me how to throw the palm ball one day in Connie Mack Stadium. I think that pitch is what I needed and had a lot to do with my success in Boston."

As a member of the Red Sox, Culp turned into a big winner with 16-, 17-, 17- and 14-victory seasons before those shoulder problems pretty much did him in. But he looks back on his time with the Phillies fondly, even the '64 team that imploded.

"I feel real honored to play with that group of guys," Culp said. "There were some great ballplayers there on that team. I wasn't able to contribute as much as I would have liked toward the end of the

Photo provided by author

#37 RAY CULP • PITCHER

Phillies, Cubs, Red Sox

Born: 8/6/1941 Elgin TX
Height: 6-0 • Weight: 200 lbs. • Bats right • Throws right
11 year Major League Career: 122-101
Phillies 4 years • Major League Debut: 1963

year in '64. But that's just baseball. Some days it's your day and others it's not. Philly was a great place for me, where a lot of us young pitchers got an opportunity. When you get the chance, you have to take advantage of it. We had a great group of players and a great bunch of guys on that team. A lot had career years that season.

"My wife and I lived in Norristown, and she was really friendly with Fran Wine, Bobby's wife. We both really loved living there."

Culp was signed by the Phillies prior to the 1959 season as an amateur free agent. On December 7, 1966 he was traded with cash to the Chicago Cubs for Dick Ellsworth.

Following baseball, Ray Culp returned to the Austin area and founded a management and investment business, 123 Inc., which was named after his lifetime batting average.

Culp is the proud father of six children, and his son Wes pitched in the Atlanta Braves organization for six years. Culp was an intense competitor who was and remains to this day a private person. But he loved playing the game of baseball.

"I pitched as hard as I could and took the ball whenever I was asked," he said. "I've always been kind of a private person who is still not very outgoing today. I haven't changed much. Everyone who knows me knows I gave everything I had. Baseball was my true love since I was a kid. It was my dream to be a major league player, and I lived my dream. Life has been great to me and my family."

WOODIE
FRYMAN

Woodrow Thompson "Woodie" Fryman was acquired by the Phillies from the Pittsburgh Pirates prior to the 1968 season along with pitchers Harold Clem, Bill Laxton and shortstop Don Money in exchange for future Hall of Fame pitcher Jim Bunning. As a rookie with the Pirates in 1966, he reeled off three consecutive shutouts en route to a 12-9 record.

After a rough sophomore season, he got right back on track with the Phillies. He stepped in and won 12 games in each of his first two seasons in Philadelphia.

"I came to Philly in '68 and got off to a good start under Gene Mauch," Fryman said. "He was the best manager I ever played for. I thought he really knew the game. His problem was his temperament. I played for him in Philly and again in Montreal."

A question that followed this hard-throwing left-hander during his career dealt with his age. Three years mysteriously were unaccounted for with the Pirates. "When Pittsburgh signed me I was 25," he admitted. "But they said I was 22. But we corrected that later."

Fryman had another good year in Philadelphia, winning 10 games in 1971, but he slumped to 4-10 the following year. A late-

PHILADELPHIA PHILLIES

WOODIE
FRYMAN

PITCHER

#35 WOODIE FRYMAN • PITCHER

Pirates, Phillies, Tigers, Expos, Cubs

Born: 4/15/1940 Ewing KY
Height: 6-2 • Weight: 205 lbs. • Bats right • Throws right
18 year Major League Career: 141-155
Phillies 5 years • Major League Debut: 1966

season change of scenery did wonders, and he helped the Detroit Tigers get into the postseason.

"I liked the time I spent in Philadelphia," he said. "I left there in 1972 when I couldn't get anybody out. Then I went to Detroit and won 10 games in two months."

He continued to pitch effectively, bouncing around from the Tigers to the Expos, Reds and Cubs. But he became a dependable relief pitcher in his second tour of duty with the Expos. From 1979 to 1983, Woodie Fryman won 24 games and saved 46 more north of the border. This veteran overcame severe arthritis in his pitching elbow and stayed in the game until he was 43, even though the Pirates may have thought he was just 40.

After his career ended, Fryman returned to his Kentucky roots and a tobacco farm.

"I have about 500 acres of land here about a half-mile from where I was raised," he said.

GENE GARBER

Gene Garber was a hard-working, side-wheeling right-hander with a corkscrew motion that he learned from Luis Tiant in Triple A that confused and confounded many a major league hitter. Although he pitched effectively for nearly two decades in the major leagues, he really came into his own with his hometown team, the Phillies, in 1974, after some chances with the Pirates and Royals.

"I grew up a Phillie fan, so it was a dream come true for me to pitch for the team," he said. "My second game in the majors with the Pirates I pitched in old Connie Mack Stadium. It was a thrill for me to play there and then later to play for the team and meet guys like Richie Ashburn and Robin Roberts. For the most part, Philadelphia treated me very well. Even when I came into town as a member of the Braves, the fans always acknowledged me as if to thank me for the effort I gave that organization."

In his five seasons in Philadelphia, Gino won 33 games out of the bullpen and saved 51 more. But if there is one game that will forever be etched in his memory as well as the fans', it was Game 3 of the NLCS against the Dodgers on October 7, 1977. Garber came into the game to hold a lead in the seventh inning and retired the first

PHILADELPHIA PHILLIES

GENE
GARBER

PITCHER

Photo © The Phillies

#26 GENE GARBER • PITCHER

Phillies, Royals, Braves, Pirates

Born: 11/13/1947 Lancaster PA
Height: 5-10 • Weight: 175 lbs. • Bats right • Throws right
19 year Major League Career: 96-113
Phillies 5 years • Major League Debut: 1969

eight batters he faced and had two outs and two strikes in the ninth inning when Vic Davalillo laid down a perfect bunt for a hit.

Unlike most of the regular season, Phillies manager Danny Ozark left Greg Luzinski in the game in left field, rather than inserting slick-fielding Jerry Martin.

Pinch hitter Manny Mota hit a fly ball the bounced off of Luzinski's glove at the wall, and the Dodgers eventually won the game, breaking the collective hearts of the Delaware Valley.

"That was one of the strangest games I've ever been in," said Garber. "It was the most memorable game I've ever been in. It was the most fun I've ever had pitching and then the most nightmarish. I got eight hitters out in a row in the seventh, eighth and ninth and then with two strikes, Davalillo laid down a perfect bunt for a hit. People ask about Mota's hit, but when he hit it I knew the game was over. The ball kept drifting, and Bull went with it and it hit his glove and he didn't catch it. That was the only time I ever saw him not catch a ball that hit his glove."

Garber later moved on to the Atlanta Braves, where he was an outstanding pitcher for a decade. He still holds the Atlanta record for career saves with 141, and his 557 games rank him third in team history, after Warren Spahn and Phil Niekro.

Even though it's been a quarter of a century, Garber will forever be remembered as the pitcher who ended Pete Rose's 44-game hitting streak on August 1, 1978. Always the competitor, Gino pitched Rose tough, striking him out on a change-up to end the game and the streak.

Immediately after the game, Rose complained that Garber pitched him like it was the seventh game of the World Series. He is correct, because that is how Gene Garber pitched everyone.

"When the Reds came to town, I hoped for an opportunity to stop him," Garber said. "I'd be less than professional if I didn't want to end the streak. Phil Niekro once told me to make every pitch like it was the last pitch I was ever going to make. That really stuck with me, and that's how I pitched Rose. I think any criticism he might have had about my pitching him the way I did may have had something to do with the fact that it was also the final out of the game and he didn't have much time to compose himself before the postgame interviews began."

Garber saved 218 games during his career using a variety of off-speed pitches. He saved 30 games for the '82 Braves, but also saved more than 10 games 11 times in his career.

Following his baseball career, Garber returned home to Elizabethtown, Pennsylvania, and became a full-time farmer. He and his brother split their partnership so that a new generation of Garbers could get involved in the family business. Now Gene and his two grown sons, Greg and Mike, own and operate 400 acres.

"I think I'd like to be remembered for my longevity and for the effort I gave," he said. "I wasn't a star, but when I was retired, there were only four active pitchers who had more games than me. I really felt that was a pretty good achievement for a small guy who didn't throw hard. I pitched every hitter like it was the bottom of the ninth inning in the seventh game of the World Series."

GREG HARRIS

Much like songstress Judy Collins's song about life, Greg Harris has looked at baseball from both sides now. A switch hitter at the plate, Harris was the only pitcher in the 20th century to throw in a major league game both as a righty and a lefty.

The last pitcher to do so before Harris was Elton "Ice Box" Chamberlain, a natural right-hander of Louisville in the American Association. On May 9, 1888, Ice Box pitched the final two scoreless innings of an 18-6 win over Kansas City left handed. More than 100 years passed before that feat was equaled by Greg Harris.

Harris's ambidextrous appearance occurred on September 28, 1995, in his final major league game, while pitching for the Montreal Expos against the Cincinnati Reds. From his usual right side, he retired Reds leadoff hitter Reggie Sanders in the ninth inning. He switched to southpaw and walked left-handed-hitting Hal Morris. Staying a lefty, Harris got Eddie Taubensee to ground out before switching to the right side again to retire Bret Boone.

A righty during his entire career, Greg Harris always had the ability to throw from the left side.

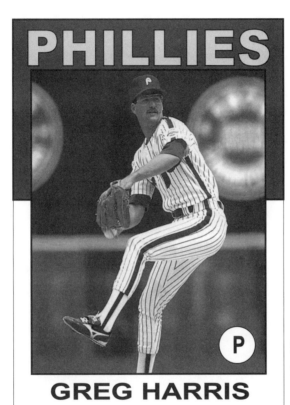

Photo © The Phillies

PHILLIES

GREG HARRIS

#33 GREG HARRIS • PITCHER
Phillies, Mets, Reds, Expos, Padres, Rangers, Red Sox, Yankees

Born: 11/2/1955 Lynwood CA
Height: 6-0 • Weight: 175 lbs. • Bats both • Throws both
15 year Major League Career: 74-90
Phillies 2 years • Major League Debut: 1981

"I always threw with both arms growing up," he said. "I used to shag balls left-handed, but in 1986 with Texas, Tom House [pitching coach] and Bobby Valentine [manager] got me working on it in August with the idea of doing it on the last weekend of the season. Valentine wanted me to be able to throw 25 out of 30 pitches for strikes, throw at least 80 mph and be able to throw a curveball. I could do all three."

But the plans went amiss when the Rangers headed into the final series against Anaheim in a playoff race. Finally in 1995, Felipe Alou of the Expos told Harris that he wanted to see him throw with both arms in the big leagues. The rest is history.

"Under the circumstances, I doubt it will ever happen again," said Harris. "I think it was quite an accomplishment for a guy who was pretty much a no-name player. I was a reliable pitcher who did a good job. I wasn't a superstar, but was a team player who made the most of my opportunities. Now I'm part of history."

The special six-finger glove that Harris had made and used in that historic game is now in the Baseball Hall of Fame.

Oh, by the way, Harris, a right-handed curveball specialist except for that one game, had a fine 15-year career. Primarily used as a reliever, Harris did start 98 games during his career. He went 13-9 in a starting role for the Red Sox in 1990 and had 11 wins the following year in a dual role.

His best season out of the bullpen was in 1986 for Texas when he won 10 games and saved 20 more. His flexibility, durability and ability to start, set up and close while pitching a few times a week made him a valuable commodity during his 15-year big-league career.

"I knew how to pitch, had a good curveball and good control," he said. "I was pretty resilient and could throw all the time. I'd pitch in 60 games and have 100-plus innings. You'd go out and throw two or three innings. I also got to pitch in the '84 World Series for the Padres against Detroit. That was probably the highlight of my career."

Harris enjoyed his time in Philadelphia. He loved the area and had some great teammates, even though the team did not fare all that well.

"Eighty-eight was an awesome year with the Phillies," he said. "I pitched real well that year and the next. I had a blast with that team. Players like Mike Schmidt, Bob Dernier, Randy Ready, Lance Parrish and Darren Daulton were outstanding. Gus Hoefling got us all in great shape. Even though we didn't play that well, we all had a good time.

"I really enjoyed the town. It has such great history."

Following his career, Greg Harris became a minor league instructor with the Tampa Bay Devil Rays and later Seattle. Feeling the desire to teach players, he opened up a pitching school and has two traveling teams. He also spends time helping out at Kennedy High School in La Palma, California.

DAROLD KNOWLES

This crafty lefty with a smooth, side-arm delivery became an outstanding reliever, accumulating 143 saves during his career. He was a big part of the Oakland bullpen during their World Series runs in the 1970s. In 1972, Darold Knowles set a record by pitching in all seven World Series games that year against the Mets. No other pitcher in the history of the game has that distinction.

Knowles broke into the majors with the Orioles in 1965 and was acquired by the Phillies that winter in exchange for outfielder Jackie Brandt and reliever Jack Baldschun. He responded with a 6-5 record with 13 saves as a 24-year-old, prompting his manager Gene Mauch to liken his courage to that of a "daylight burglar."

Even though he was dealt to the Washington Senators that winter so the Phillies could fill an outfield hole with Don Lock, he appreciates his lone year as a Phillie.

"The year I played with the Phillies was my rookie year, so a lot of really important things happened," he said. "Richie Allen was on that team, and when he came up to the plate, everything stopped because everybody wanted to watch him. I played with some great players that year, like Jim Bunning, Dick Groat, Larry Jackson, Bill

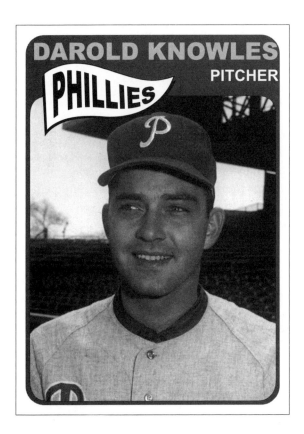

#32 DAROLD KNOWLES • PITCHER

Phillies, A's, Senators, Cubs, Rangers, Expos, Cards

Born: 12/9/1941 Brunswick MO
Height: 6-0 • Weight: 190 lbs. • Bats left • Throws left
16 year Major League Career: 66-74
Phillies 1 year • Major League Debut: 1965

White and Chris Short. That was a helluva team for a rookie to break in with, and they all took me under their wing and took care of me.

"Playing with so many great veterans probably helped me a lot later in my career. I was a brash, cocky little guy, which was why I became a closer. These guys helped you know what to do in certain situations and, more importantly, what not to do. If I messed up, there were eight guys there to let me know."

He didn't mess up very often, as he was tied for 13th in career saves when he retired. After leaving the Phillies, Knowles had some good years in Washington including a weird season in 1970 when he went 2-14, but had 27 saves and an outstanding 2.04 ERA in 71 games.

He had four fine years with the A's before moving on to the Cubs, Rangers, Expos and Cards before hanging them up in 1980 after 16 seasons in the show.

Following his career, he has been a minor league pitching instructor with the Cardinals and Phillies as well as a major league coach with the Phils. For the past three years, he has mentored the young Pirates prospects with the Nashville Sounds.

BILL LAXTON

Bill Laxton was a local guy who had the opportunity to pitch for his favorite team. The flame-throwing southpaw had great stuff, but like many left-handers, had trouble finding the strike zone with it.

A seventh-round draft choice by the Pittsburgh Pirates in 1966, Laxton was traded to the Phillies in December of 1967 with pitchers Harold Clem, Woodie Fryman and infielder Don Money in exchange for future Hall of Fame pitcher Jim Bunning. While he appeared in just two games out of the bullpen for the Phillies, Laxton was living large, living his childhood dream of not just pitching in the major leagues, but wearing a Phillies uniform.

"I came up to the Phillies with Greg Luzinski when we were both playing at Reading," Laxton said. "Then here we were playing in Connie Mack Stadium. I got in for a couple of innings. The first batter I faced in the majors was Richie Hebner, and I hit him on the butt with a pitch. He said that it really hurt.

"I grew up in the area, and the Phillies were my team. You watch guys like Dalrymple and Callison, and the next thing you know, you're at spring training with them."

PHILADELPHIA PHILLIES

BILL
LAXTON

PITCHER

Photo provided by author

#45 BILL LAXTON • PITCHER

Phillies, Padres, Tigers, Mariners, Indians

Born: 1/5/1948 Camden NJ
Height: 6-1 • Weight: 190 lbs. • Bats left • Throws left
5 year Major League Career: 3-10
Phillies 1 year • Major League Debut: 1970

His time with the Phillies was short, however, as that winter the Padres acquired him in the Rule V draft. He went 0-2 in 18 games in 1971, plagued by his questionable control. Banished to the minor league for two seasons, Laxton pitched in 30 games for the '74 Padres with an 0-1 record.

"I was a starter in the minors and wound up as a long man in the majors," he said. "When you get called up as a long man, you don't get much of a chance. I had a little trouble with my control. I just wish I had gotten it together a little sooner."

After playing in the New York Mets organization for one season, Laxton was dealt along with Rusty Staub to the Detroit Tigers for Mickey Lolich and Billy Baldwin in December 1975.

But an 0-5 record with the Tigers turned this former top prospect into a suspect. But after being selected by the Seattle Mariners in the expansion draft, he finally started to settle in, going 3-2 in 43 games with three saves. He did get credit for the first win in Seattle Mariners history. Arm problems then ensued, and Bill Laxton was done after the 1977 season with a 3-10 career mark.

His son, Brett, was 0-2 for the A's and Royals in 1999 and 2000.

For the last 18 years, Bill Laxton has been an operator for the Public Works Department in Audubon, New Jersey.

JIM LONBORG

Gentleman Jim Lonborg was a popular player who made a name for himself as a member of the 1967 Boston Red Sox pennant-winning team. He led the staff with a 22-9 record and a league-leading 246 strikeouts, earning Cy Young award honors. He hurled a one-hitter in the World Series, beating the Cards 5-0. He also threw a three-hitter en route to a 3-1 win in Game 5, but lost Game 7, pitching on only two days' rest.

After breaking his leg in a skiing accident that winter, Lonborg was not nearly as effective over the next few years. He went 6-10 with the Bosox in 1968 and 7-11 the following year. But after a 10-7 campaign in 1971, Lonborg was dealt to Milwaukee and had resurrected his career with a 14-12 season with a 2.82 ERA.

That winter he was traded to the Phillies along with Ken Brett, Ken Sanders and Earl Stephenson in exchange for Don Money, John Vukovich and Billy Champion. The change in leagues turned out to be a difficult adjustment, but the Phillies made Lonborg feel right at home right from the start.

"I had a good seven years down there," he said from his Massachusetts home about his tenure in Philadelphia. "I had not heard a single thing about the Phillies. In the American League you only think

PHILADELPHIA PHILLIES

JIM
LONBORG

PITCHER

#41 JIM LONBORG • PITCHER
Phillies, Red Sox, Brewers

Born: 4/16/1942 Santa Maria CA
Height: 6-5 • Weight: 210 lbs. • Bats right • Throws right
15 year Major League Career: 157-137
Phillies 7 years • Major League Debut: 1965

about American League teams. You never really get a chance to know the National League. But the Phillies had great owners in the Carpenters and a great general manager in Paul Owens. He called me the night I got traded.

"Philadelphia was a very pleasant change of scenery. I felt good about myself and my career after having a good year in Milwaukee. I liked where my career was headed."

After a bit of a slow start in Philadelphia, Lonborg won over the fans and earned the respect of his teammates as he won 13, 17, 8, 18 and 11 games between 1973 and 1977. He also flirted with a no-hitter in the 1977 NLCS against the Cincinnati Reds.

The move to the Phillies not only was a good career move for the classy right-hander, but was also a wonderful experience for Jim and Rosemary Lonborg and their family.

"I think the fans saw how hard I worked to make the adjustment from the American to the National League and appreciated the effort," he said. "Our lives really took shape down there. The people knew about our adopting children and then having our first [biological] child. We were really blessed as a family in Philadelphia."

Following an 8-10 campaign in 1978, Lonborg no longer fit into the team's plans and was released in June of 1979 after going 0-1 in just four games.

He called it quits and went to the University of Massachusetts and Tufts Dentistry School and became a dentist in 1983, which has been his career since. Jim Lonborg enjoyed his baseball career and looks back to his experiences in Philadelphia happily.

"I look back with great pride being able to play 15 years in the big leagues," he said. "I worked very hard to keep in shape and had a pretty darn good career. But when I look at our family, I think of Philly. We left there with five beautiful children that weren't there prior to Philly. That was the gift that Philadelphia gave us. It's something we'll never forget."

TOM QUALTERS

Tom "Money Bags" Qualters was a bonus baby who fell victim to the rule that forced major league teams to keep such players on the major league roster. He appeared in just one game his rookie season of 1953, pitching just one-third of an inning. After spending the next three years in the minor leagues, he made just six appearances with the '57 Phillies, pitching only seven innings even though he had become a solid relief pitcher in the minors.

"That crazy rule basically took two years out of my career," he said. "They had the fear that if they used you and you didn't play well that it would ruin your confidence. It was very frustrating. That was the dumbest rule I ever saw. Because of that I never felt I belonged up there in the major leagues."

In 1958, Qualters pitched in one more game for the Phillies before being purchased by the Chicago White Sox in April.

"My time in Philadelphia was bittersweet," he said. "A couple of the managers I had there didn't seem to feel I was that great a prospect. In addition to that, some guys didn't think you belonged there either because they felt that you were taking someone else's place who could help the club. But Jim Konstany, Curt Simmons, Robin Roberts and Earl Torgeson really treated me well."

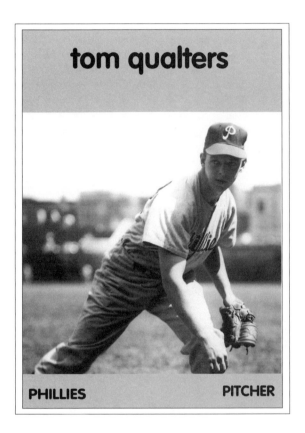

tom qualters

PHILLIES   PITCHER

#33 TOM QUALTERS • PITCHER

Phillies, White Sox

Born: 4/1/1935 McKeesport PA
Height: 6-0 • Weight: 190 lbs. • Bats right • Throws right
4 year Major League Career: 0-0
Phillies 3 years • Major League Debut: 1953

The highlight of Qualters's major league career was the remainder of the 1958 season with the White Sox. He appeared in 26 games and pitched very well in 43 innings. White Sox manager Al Lopes was so impressed with what he saw that he told Qualters that he would be the team's fifth starter in 1959. It finally appeared that Tom Qualters would get his chance.

But as luck would have it, he suffered an arm injury in 1959, which kept him from ever finding out just how good he'd be.

However briefly, Qualters lived his major league dream. After baseball, he achieved another childhood dream by spending 35 years as a conservation law enforcement officer near Pittsburgh. His son, Tom Jr., followed in his footsteps and currently also works in conservation.

STEVE RIDZIK

This right-hander, who spent most of his career as a journeyman-type reliever and spot starter, made his major league debut with the 1950 Whiz Kids team at the age of 21. While he appeared in just one game with a three-inning stint that year, he showed that he had what it took to pitch major league baseball.

Following a year in the minor leagues, Ridzik returned to the Phils in 1952, going 4-2 in 24 games. His winningest big-league season followed in 1953, when he went 9-6 in 42 games. His Phillies career ended when he was dealt to Cincinnati in a major trade in April of 1955 along with Smoky Burgess and Stan Palys in exchange for Andy Seminick, Glen Gorbous and Jim Greengrass.

"The Phillies organization was a great organization," Ridzik said. "Mr. Bob Carpenter and Mrs. Carpenter really cared about the ballplayers, and they treated us all like family. I don't think you have that attitude today in baseball.

"The city of Philadelphia has always been good to me. It's known as a tough city on athletes, but the fans there were wonderful to me. They always treated me well. I have so many great memories of people like Eddie Waitkus and Bill Nicholson, who took very good care of me when I was a young kid coming up.

#20 STEVE RIDZIK • PITCHER
Phillies, Reds, Giants, Indians, Senators

Born: 4/29/1929 Yonkers NY
Height: 5-11 • Weight: 170 lbs. • Bats right • Throws right
12 year Major League Career: 39-38
Phillies 6 years • Major League Debut: 1950

"I'll never forget the time they both came up to me in the outfield when I was shagging fly balls on opening day and they shook my hand and said, 'Congratulations. You're a major league ball player.' Those two guys really looked out for me."

Ridzik pitched for the Reds, Giants and Indians before a five-year exodus to the minor leagues. After bouncing around and never losing sight of his big-league dreams, he caught on with the 1963 Washington Senators. Ridzik had three fine years in Washington, winning 16 games and saving 11 more. He appeared in 63 games out of the bullpen for the '65 Senators, his career high.

After his second tour of duty with the Phillies, albeit a brief one in 1966, Steve worked as a regional manager in the food brokerage business in Washington D.C., selling to U.S. military commissaries all over the world.

He is now enjoying retirement in Bradenton, Florida.

"I've been retired since 1986," Ridzik said. "I had worked in the food industry for 20 years. It's the greatest life in the world being retired. And they pay for it."

ROBIN ROBERTS

This Hall of Fame right-hander began his big-league career in Phila-delphia in 1948 at the age of 21. Following a 7-9 rookie cam-paign, Robin Roberts began a string of 12 consecutive seasons with double-digit win totals, including six consecutive 20-win seasons and a seventh with 19 victories. He led the league in wins with 28 in 1952 as well as the next three years in which he won 23 games. During that span of 20-win seasons, this workhorse also threw at least 304 in-nings six times.

Roberts suffered through a 10-22 season in 1957, but rebounded with 17 and 15 wins the next two years. But after a 1-10 1961 season, he was purchased by the New York Yankees in October, who released him the following May. Robin Roberts then signed on with the Balti-more Orioles, where he once again found success and fooled his crit-ics who thought he was through.

Robbie has nothing but fond memories of his years in Philadel-phia, where he and his wife raised their family.

"It was a wonderful time for me," he said. "We lived there for 27 years. From 1948 to 1955, we were a real good ball club. We were solid, and I was winning 20 games every year."

robin roberts

PHILLIES   PITCHER

#36 ROBIN ROBERTS • PITCHER
Phillies, Orioles, Astros, Cubs

Born: 9/30/1926 Springfield IL
Height: 6-0 • Weight: 190 lbs. • Bats right • Throws right
19 year Major League Career: 286-245
Phillies 14 years • Major League Debut: 1948

After four years with Baltimore, he also pitched for Houston and the Cubs, where he ended his 19-year major league career.

"At the end of my career with the Cubs, they asked me to be a pitching coach for them," he said. "At that point in my life, I wanted to stay with my family. If I could have still pitched, I would have done it. But I thought that coaching was overstated and I just didn't want to continue traveling for that.

"After my playing days ended, I was in the investment business for 11 years and then coached the University of South Florida at Tampa for eight years," Roberts said.

"Now I'm retired and make appearances. I've also written a couple of books."

Robin Roberts, one of the greatest pitchers to ever play for the Phillies, was inducted into the Baseball Hall of Fame in 1976.

CHRIS SHORT

C hris Short was an outstanding pitcher for the Phillies through-out the 1960s, winning 17, 18, 19 and 20 games during that decade. When he won 20 games in 1966, he became the first Phillies left-hander to reach that mark since Eppa Rixey was a 22-game winner in 1916.

A workhorse who always kept his team in the game, Short tied what was then a post-1900 National League record by striking out 18 New York Mets in 15 innings. The game ended in a 0-0 tie.

Nicknamed "Styles" because of his modest collection of cloth-ing early in his career, he was nothing but stylish on the mound. He and Jim Bunning almost pitched the Phillies to the 1964 pennant, only to see the club collapse in the final two weeks of the season.

While the Phillies' fortunes went south after the '64 season, Short became better each year. He followed up his 17-9 record in the season that catcher Gus Triandos called "the year of the blue snow" with an 18-11 1965. He then followed with his 20-win campaign in '66. Short tailed off to 9-11 in 1968 before having his final big season of 19-13 in 1968.

"Chris had a rubber arm," said outfielder Doug Clemens. "I don't think he ever had a sore arm. I liked him a lot. He was a very

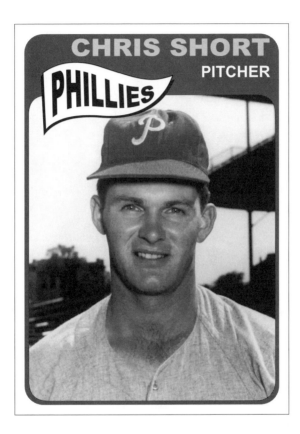

#41 CHRIS SHORT • PITCHER
Phillies, Brewers

Born: 9/19/1937 Milford DE • Died: 8/1/1991 Wilmington DE
Height: 6-4 • Weight: 205 lbs. • Bats right • Throws left
15 year Major League Career: 135-132
Phillies 14 years • Major League Debut: 1959

unique guy, probably a little naive. But he was a great pitcher and a tough competitor. He was a lot of fun. He even liked to think that he was a pretty good hitter, even though he was not."

After seven seasons as the top southpaw on the staff, a serious back injury cost him most of the 1969 season. He came back the following season, going 9-16, but was obviously not the same pitcher. Short finished up his career with Milwaukee in 1973 going 3-5.

Short was signed by the Phillies as an amateur free agent prior to the 1957 season. He was released on October 26, 1972.

He holds the most pitching records by a Delawarean and was considered the greatest left-handed pitcher in Phillies history before Steve Carlton.

He died in 1991 after suffering a brain aneurysm and lapsing into a coma in October 1988 at his insurance business.

CURT SIMMONS

Curt Simmons was one of the youngest members of the 1950 Whiz Kids team, helping them capture the National League pennant with a 17-8 season. Unfortunately for him and the team, his season was cut short by military service. As a result, the left-hander missed out on an opportunity to pitch in the World Series against the New York Yankees.

A native of Egypt, Pennsylvania, not far from Allentown, Simmons would have loved to have had the opportunity to pitch in the Fall Classic.

"I was a local guy, and we had some good years and a few bad ones," he said. "The Whiz Kids team was great, but I missed the last month of the season serving in the military. As a result, I didn't pitch in the World Series."

Simmons sported a herky-jerky motion on the mound that often baffled opposing hitters, but he blames his pitching motion for problems that caused a hip and knee replacement.

Simmons was signed by the Phillies as an amateur free agent prior to the 1947 season. He was released on May 20, 1960.

#28 CURT SIMMONS • PITCHER
Phillies, Cards, Cubs, Angels

Born: 5/19/29 Egypt PA
Height: 6-0 • Weight: 187 lbs. • Bats left • Throws left
20 year Major League Career: 193-183
Phillies 13 years • Major League Debut: 1947

In the span from 1950 to 1957, Curt Simmons won 96 games. He had a league-high six shutouts in 1952. The hard-throwing southpaw won 16 in 1953 despite missing a month of the season after slicing off part of his left big toe in a lawn mower accident. The following year, he came right back with 15 wins.

After he suffered through arm miseries in 1959, the Phillies released him in 1960 after 12 seasons with the club. That move still hurts decades later.

"I spent 12 full seasons with the Phillies and at the end, they released me when I was not quite 31," he said. "They released me at midnight in San Francisco, which was a pretty rotten thing."

Simmons rebounded and signed with the St. Louis Cardinals. He posted 62 wins for them in five seasons, disproving the Phillies' belief that he was through. His 18-9 season in 1964 helped the Cards to the World Series, ironically the same year of the infamous Phillies collapse.

"Pitching for the Cardinals in '64 was great," Simmons said. "I finally got to pitch in a World Series after not being able to in 1950. It was quite a thrill coming off the old scrap heap."

His old teammate, Robin Roberts, saw just how effective the lefty was with St. Louis.

"Curt did a marvelous job with the Cardinals," he said.

Simmons has been an owner of the Limekiln Golf Course in Ambler since 1965. He still enjoys his involvement there.

"I'm just a farmer-type guy," he said. "I wasn't really equipped to do much after my playing career ended. But I got involved with the golf course and really enjoyed it. I came from upstate Pennsylvania, and when I got married, we bought a house in the Philadelphia suburbs."

MORRIE STEEVENS

After being signed as an amateur free agent by the Chicago Cubs in 1958, this left-hander made a name for himself in the minor leagues. In 1962 he won 15 games for San Antonio in the Texas League. That season earned him his first taste of the major leagues as a Cub.

He appeared in his big-league career-high 12 games, going 0-1 as a 21-year-old. Following one more season with the Chicago organization, he was acquired by the Phillies prior to the 1964 campaign and assigned to the Boom Boom Travelers, their power-hitting Triple A team in Little Rock. Playing for future Phillies manager Frank Lucchesi, Steevens had an 8-1 record, including a no-hitter. His future seemed bright, and he had the opportunity to appear in four games for the big club that season. But much like in Chicago, most of his appearances were situations where the young lefty was expected to get one batter out. After starting in the minor leagues, it was a tough adjustment.

"I didn't play that much," he said. "They always brought me in to face left-handed batters, and I didn't have a whole lot of luck. Pitching to Stan Musial, my idol as a kid, was a highlight of my career, though."

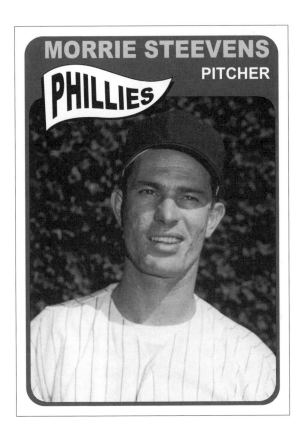

#58, 47, 23 MORRIE STEEVENS • PITCHER

Phillies, Cubs

Born: 10/7/1940 Salem IL
Height: 6-2 • Weight: 175 lbs. • Bats left • Throws left
3 year Major League Career: 0-2
Phillies 2 years • Major League Debut: 1962

Steevens also pitched for the Phillies in 1965, going 0-1 in six outings. Again, the former starter threw less than three innings in his six games.

Back in the minor leagues, he then developed arm problems and needed surgery. The success he had at the minor league level never followed him to the major leagues. If he had the opportunity to be used as he had been in the minor leagues, things might have turned out differently. But his arm miseries ended his career before he turned 30.

"I had to have surgery on my arm," he said. "Then I went to San Diego, and they released me."

After baseball, this southpaw worked as a county tax assessor and is still employed as a tax consultant for a law firm. He lives in San Antonio, Texas.

ERSKINE THOMASON

Erskine Thomason is one of those names that is hard to forget. After being drafted in the 22nd round of the 1970 amateur draft, he worked his way through the Phillies' minor league system and was considered a top pitching prospect. There were numerous reasons that Thomason was considered on the fast track to a career as a major league starter.

While pitching for Erskine College, this hurler struck out all 18 batters in a game against Wofford. After turning pro, he was a 12-game winner for the '73 Reading Phillies. The future seemed to hold nothing but good things.

Thomason was promoted to the Phillies at the end of the 1974 season and pitched in one game. They could not have asked for more, as he responded with a scoreless inning, including a strikeout. But then, for some reason, he no longer seemed to fit into the Phillies' plans for the future. Many people have wondered what happened to this once impressive pitching prospect's career.

"I've asked myself that a thousand times," said Thomason. "After my glorious time in the big leagues, one game, I went back to our Triple A affiliate in Toledo in '75 and pitched out of the bullpen for

PHILADELPHIA PHILLIES

ERSKINE
THOMASON

PITCHER

Photo provided by Erskine Thomason

#48 ERSKINE THOMASON • PITCHER

Phillies

Born: 8/13/1948 Laurens SC
Height: 6-1 • Weight: 190 lbs. • Bats right • Throws right
1 year Major League Career: 0-0
Phillies 1 year • Major League Debut: 1974

Jim Bunning. But I was going nowhere, and I had two young children and decided to retire."

After working out of baseball for a couple of years, Thomason approached the team about a coaching position, but found himself pitching for one last season for the Reading Phillies. He then became a coach for the Phillies and then a roving minor league pitching instructor for the Cubs. But the travel kept him away from home more than he wanted, and Erskine Thomason gave up baseball for good in 1987. But his memories are very fond ones.

"You never forget the relationships you have with the guys and the camaraderie," he said. "You always try to keep up and stay in touch with those guys."

He is now the sales manager for Fairway Outdoor Advertising in Greenville, South Carolina, and lives in his hometown of Laurens.

WAYNE TWITCHELL

This big, hard-throwing right-hander was an enigma during most of his career. His stuff was outstanding, but his control problems limited his success in the big leagues. His best year was 1973, when he went 13-9 for the Phillies with a 2.50 ERA and made the All-Star team. It was ironic that he made that squad as a Phillie since he was a fan of the team since childhood.

"I grew up in Portland, and all of my friends rooted for the Yankees," he said. "But I had always sort of been attached to Robin Roberts. My first glove was a Robin Roberts glove, and I wore number 36 all through high school."

After going 1-0 in six scoreless outings for the 1971 Phillies, Twitchell went 5-9 in his first full big-league season the following year as a spot starter and reliever. What followed was his 13-win season, but a serious knee injury stalled his progress as a pitcher.

It seemed as though Twitchell had made the turn with his breakout year in 1973, but his knee injury resulted in a five-hour operation and he never came close to matching those numbers again.

He went 14-25 over the next three years in Philadelphia. The Phillies organization and Philadelphia fans have had questionable repu-

PHILADELPHIA PHILLIES

WAYNE
TWITCHELL

PITCHER

#33 WAYNE TWITCHELL • PITCHER

Phillies, Brewers, Expos, Mets, Mariners

Born: 3/10/1948 Portland OR
Height: 6-6 • Weight: 220 lbs. • Bats right • Throws right
10 year Major League Career: 48-65
Phillies 7 years • Major League Debut: 1970

tations. But as far as Wayne Twitchell is concerned, both were tremendous.

"It was a treat to play for the Phillies," he said. "The organization is the best in baseball. Players I knew from other teams were jealous of us. The Carpenter family was first class all the way.

"As far as the city is concerned, they've got the best sandwiches in the world. The fans were extremely knowledgeable about the game. I actually played a whole season without being booed. We had a pretty good team, and we were expected to win just about every night. We also drew about 30,000 season ticket holders. It was very exciting playing there. When I was on the mound, if I heard the crowd when I was pitching, that meant that I wasn't concentrating enough. I tried to void it from my mind.

"As a competitor, I can honestly say that in the years I played in Philadelphia, there was not one player who didn't give 100 percent."

After his seven-year tenure with the Phillies was over, Twitchell also pitched for the Expos, Mets and Mariners for another three years with a 15-22 record. He was done after the '79 campaign.

Since his career ended, Wayne Twitchell has worked in real estate and for more than a dozen years has volunteered as a pitching coach for a local school in Portland, Oregon.

FRED WENZ

Fireball Freddie Wenz could throw hard and was a strikeout pitcher who showed lots of promise in his three-year journey in the big-leagues. Originally signed by the San Francisco Giants, he enjoyed little success as a starter early in his minor league career. But after joining the Boston Red Sox organization, he found his niche out of the bullpen.

While pitching for Pittsfield in 1965, Wenz struck out 129 batters in 102 innings. In Toronto in 1967, he fanned 76 batters in 60 innings. And in 1968 and '69, he pitched in 61 games with 30 saves. Phillies general manager John Quinn sent reliever Gary Wagner to the Red Sox in exchange for Wenz and Mike Jackson prior to the 1970 season.

As a player who grew up near Philadelphia, Fireball Freddie was thrilled to have the chance to pitch with the Phillies after nine big-league appearances with the Red Sox over a two-year span.

"I loved being with the Phillies," he said. "I only lived an hour from Connie Mack Stadium in Somerville, New Jersey. I wouldn't trade my experiences in baseball for the world. I gave up college to pursue baseball. When I came up it was with people like Larry Bowa, Denny Doyle and Oscar Gamble. The Phillies had guys like Chris

Photo provided by author

#32 FRED WENZ • PITCHER
Phillies, Red Sox

Born: 8/26/1941 Bound Brook NJ
Height: 6-3 • Weight: 214 lbs. • Bats right • Throws right
3 year Major League Career: 3-0
Phillies 1 year • Major League Debut: 1968

Short, Jim Bunning and Joe Hoerner on the team. I just wish I had gotten there sooner."

His best year was his last, going 2-0 with the Phillies with one save in 22 games in 1970. He seemed like a sure fire bet to contend for the closer's spot in 1971. But that season that showed so much promise, he vanished from the game.

Contract negotiations with Phillies' general manager John Quinn frustrated Wenz, who decided the take an offer outside of baseball, even though he was still in his prime.

"I got into a contract dispute with John Quinn, who was ridiculous," he said. "I went 2-0 with a save, and he tried to cut my salary. He'd argue over a thousand dollars. I was acquired in a trade and was actually making more than Ray Culp and Grant Jackson, who had already established themselves. Then, I got an offer out of baseball that I just couldn't refuse. In those days, money in baseball was not that good."

Although disappointed about how his career ended, Wenz learned much from the game and credits his baseball days for preparing him for the business world.

"Because of baseball, I developed a personality that was great for sales," he said. "As a liquor salesman I was right up there at the top. All of my baseball background really helped me to succeed."

And succeed he has. Fireball Freddie Wenz worked as a liquor salesman for 18 years and now owns a company, Garden Oaks Specialties, in Bound Brook, New Jersey. The company deals in storage sheds, gazebos, swing sets, playhouses and ponds. In addition, Wenz owns a snowmobile lodge in Northern New York.

In retrospect, maybe tight-fisted John Quinn did Fireball a favor. Fireball Freddie and Darrell Brandon were the last two Phillies to wear number 32 before Hall of Fame pitcher Steve Carlton.

RICK WISE

This hard-throwing right-hander broke into the major leagues as an 18-year-old with the '64 Phillies, going 5-3 in 25 games. Wise made his first big-league start on June 21st of that year in the second game of a doubleheader. In the first game, Jim Bunning pitched a perfect game against the New York Mets. Wise then held the Mets hitless into the sixth inning of the nightcap.

After spending a little more than a year in Triple A, Wise was back to stay in 1966. He soon established himself as the staff ace, winning 45 games between 1969 and 1971.

In June of '71, en route to a 17-win season, Wise made history when he pitched a no-hitter in Cincinnati against the Reds. Not only did he hold the Big Red Machine hitless, but he became the only pitcher in the history of the game to hit two home runs while throwing a no-hitter. For trivia buffs, Wise smacked his round-trippers against Ross Grimsley and Clay Carroll.

Following that season, Wise was involved in a contract dispute with Phillies general manager John Quinn. In a blockbuster deal that was not popular in Philadelphia at the time, Quinn sent Wise packing to St. Louis in exchange for left-hander Steve Carlton, who was also involved in a contract dispute following a 20-9 season. While

#18, 38 RICK WISE • PITCHER

Phillies, Cards, Red Sox, Indians, Padres

Born: 9/13/1945 Jackson MI
Height: 6-2 • Weight: 195 lbs. • Bats right • Throws right
18 year Major League Career: 188-181
Phillies 7 years • Major League Debut: 1964

Carlton got much publicity as he began to carve his Hall of Fame career, Wise went on to win 113 games following the trade.

"I don't have any bad feelings about the trade," Wise said. "Steve is a good friend of mine. But if I hadn't been good enough, the trade wouldn't have been made. The Cards didn't get hamburger in return."

He won 32 games in two seasons in St. Louis before being traded to Boston in exchange for outfielder Reggie Smith. He went 19-12 for the 1975 Bosox, helping them win the American League pennant. Wise was the winning pitcher in the World Series game that the Red Sox won over the Reds with Carlton Fisk's dramatic home run.

After four years in Boston, Wise moved to the Cleveland Indians, where he went 15-10 in 1979.

He then signed a big contract with the San Diego Padres, where he finished his big-league career in 1982. Although he had an outstanding major league career, Wise fell short of two records he wanted dearly. He wanted to play in the majors for 20 years, falling just a couple shy. The big right-hander also hoped to win 200 big-league games, missing by just 12.

"The 200 wins I wanted real bad," Wise said. "I made those goals when I was 17 years old and came real close. I know I could have done it if I had gotten the chance.

"I always gave my best and was a student of the game. I was a good all-around ballplayer."

For the past 18 years, Wise has been a minor league pitching coach for a number of organizations.

Chapter 2

INFIELDERS

RALPH CABALLERO

R alph Joseph "Putsy" Caballero spent his entire major league career with the Phillies, primarily as a reserve infielder. He did play in 113 games in 1948, boasting a respectable .245 average. But the utility man has become famous for two things. He was the youngest player ever to play third base in major league baseball at the age of 16, on September 14, 1944. And then, he is also renowned because of his nickname.

"Where I grew up in Louisiana at Sacred Heart Grammar School, everybody had a nickname," Caballero said. "My brother Raymond was known as Rainbow. And for some reason, they started to call me Putsy. That's who I've been ever since."

Although he had his best season in 1948, Caballero was a valuable player, hitting .279 the following year, and played in 46 games for the Whiz Kids team. His final big-league season was 1952, when he hit a respectable .238. After his major league career was through, Putsy continued to play in the International League with Baltimore and Syracuse before retiring after the 1955 season.

"After baseball I went into pest control," he said. "Al Hirt and Pete Fountain worked with us because they got tired of traveling. We worked for A&M Pest Control, also known as Miller the Killer. After

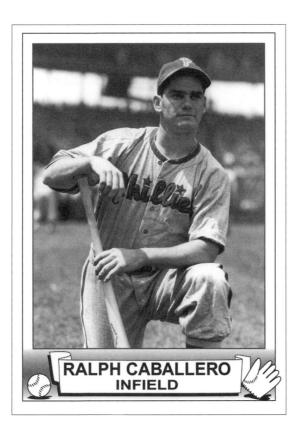

RALPH CABALLERO
INFIELD

#3 RALPH "PUTSY" CABALLERO • INFIELD

Phillies

Born: 11/05/1927 New Orleans LA
Height: 5-11 • Weight: 175 lbs. • Bats right • Throws right
8 year Major League Career • .228 avg. • 1 HR • 40 RBI
Phillies 8 years • Major League Debut: 1944

five years or so, I started my own business, DA, or deadly action pest control."

That's where he remained until his retirement in 1997. Caballero has fond memories of his time in Philadelphia.

"We all lived near Shibe Park at 21st and Lehigh," he said. "There was a great restaurant, San Framo's, that we'd eat at almost every night. They were wonderful people. They never charged me a penny because they thought I was Italian. For five years, I didn't have the heart to tell them I wasn't.

"Playing in the '50 World Series was the highlight of my career. Bob Carpenter asked us where we wanted to celebrate after we won the pennant in New York. We all said that we wanted to come back to Philadelphia. There must have been 300,000 fans at the train station. That was really something. You had to see that town."

Caballero continues to enjoy his retirement in Metairie. He is still well known in baseball circles for being a great card player, specializing in the game of hearts. He once said that he'd play baseball for a dollar a year, as long as he could play cards.

CLAY DALRYMPLE

This durable backstop was the Phillies' regular catcher throughout most of the 1960s, having his most productive season in 1962, when he hit .276. Blessed with a strong arm and a quick release behind the plate, Clay Dalrymple was a fine defensive player who always played hard and could be counted on to get some crucial hits to keep innings alive. He could also block home plate with the best of them. Needless to say, his abilities were appreciated by the Phillies' pitching staff.

"I loved pitching to Clay," said former teammate Ray Culp. "He was a great competitor who had a real nice, quick release. I just wish I could have helped him a little more by holding runners on better."

Dalrymple was drafted by the Phillies from the Milwaukee Braves on November 30, 1959 in the Rule V draft. On January 20, 1969, he was traded to the Baltimore Orioles in exchange for Ron Stone.

Clay hit .238 for the infamous 1964 squad, with six home runs and 46 RBIs. He was in the midst of the Phillies swoon that September. Like everyone else, he has some thoughts on the subject.

#11 CLAY DALRYMPLE • INFIELD

Phillies, Orioles

Born: 12/3/1936 Chico CA
Height: 6-0 • Weight: 199 lbs. • Bats left • Throws right
12 year Major League Career • .233 avg. • 55 HR • 327 RBI
Phillies 9 years • Major League Debut: 1960

"There's been a lot of finger pointing over the years," Dalrymple said. "Everybody has to take part of the blame. It was a combination of events that culminated in us dropping the ball. Frank Thomas broke his hand at a time when he was giving us a big lift. But he got hurt, and Gene Mauch pitched Jim Bunning and Chris Short every other day. He gave up on Ray Culp and Art Mahaffey. No matter what we did, we couldn't win. It was the kind of situation where even when we played really well, we got beat."

Dalrymple played with the Phillies through the 1968 season, after which he was sent to the Baltimore Orioles. He tenure in Philadelphia is something he'll never forget, and many young fans grew up watching and learning the game from his TV show, *The Clay Dalrymple Show*, which aired before day telecasts.

"I had a good time playing for the Phillies," Dalrymple said. "I thought that the general manager, John Quinn, was weak, but I was not disappointed in the city of Philadelphia. I met an awful lot of nice people there. I have a lot of interest in history, and that's Philadelphia's forte. After I left there I got to three World Series in a row with the Orioles."

He later finished up with the Orioles, with whom he reached three World Series and has a perfect 2-for-2 record as a hitter in the Fall Classic. After his playing days ended, he worked as a regional sales manager for a plumbing company in Delaware and later in the food service industry.

Sadly, Clay has lost two wives, but he has a new lady in his life. They enjoy hunting and fishing in Gold Beach, Oregon.

TERRY HARMON

Terry Harmon was the classic utility player during his 10-year stay with the Phillies. He was a versatile ballplayer with the ability to play numerous positions. Equally important, he understood his role and didn't complain about coming in off of the bench. A classic contact hitter who choked high up on the bat, he had the ability to take advantage of his strengths as a ballplayer and not try to be something he wasn't.

As a result, he hit just four home runs in his career. But power wasn't his game. Versatility, flexibility and a great attitude made Terry Harmon a valuable member of the organization.

"Playing for the Phillies was wonderful," he said. "But I don't regret not getting the chance to play every day. After a while though, you kind of settle into your role."

Harmon was drafted by the Phillies on June 8, 1965 in the fifth round of the amateur draft. On April 6, 1978, he was released.

Harmon never played in more than the 87 games he appeared in as a rookie in 1969, hitting .239. He improved to .248 the following season before having a subpar 1971. But he rebounded with a fine season in '72, hitting .284, tying his career high with two home runs in 73 games.

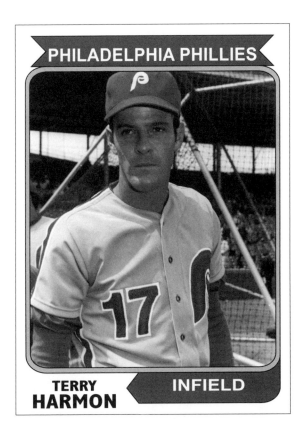

PHILADELPHIA PHILLIES

TERRY
HARMON

INFIELD

#17 TERRY HARMON • INFIELD
Phillies

Born: 4/12/1944 Toledo OH
Height: 6-2 • Weight: 180 lbs. • Bats right • Throws right
10 year Major League Career • .233 avg. • 4 HR • 72 RBI
Phillies 10 years • Major League Debut: 1967

He continued to be a dependable backup, hitting his career-high .295 in 1976, before hitting under .200 the following year. Harmon was released at spring training in 1978.

Following his retirement, he got involved in the cable television industry at just the right time. It provided for a smooth transition from baseball.

"I got involved in cable TV after baseball," Harmon said. "I worked with PRISM in sales and marketing for five years. Then after that I worked with Guide Publications and QVC for 13 years. Most recently, I've been with ACN TV working in promotions. The cable industry was a good industry to get into after baseball."

Harmon will always be remembered for his great attitude as a team player. He was accepted and appreciated by the fans, and a quarter of a century later still looks fondly upon his time with the Phillies. The Harmons remained in the area, making their home in Medford, New Jersey.

"Playing for the Phillies was phenomenal," he said. "You are doing something you wanted to do as a kid. We fell in love with the area. It's a great place to live and raise kids."

TOMMY HUTTON

This slick-fielding first baseman could never crack the Dodgers' lineup with Wes Parker at first base, although he did hit .271 in 16 games in 1969. The Phillies acquired him in exchange for Larry Hisle prior to the 1972 season.

Hutton was a fine performer and popular player during his years in Philadelphia. In his first full season in the major leagues with the Phillies in 1972, he hit .260 in 134 games. The following year, he hit .263 in 106 games. But it became apparent that as valuable as Tommy Hutton was to the team, he was considered to be more of a role player by management rather than an everyday player. While this is a tough adjustment for many players to make, Hutton was always the consummate professional who made the most of every opportunity he had, regardless of his role.

"Even though I didn't start regularly, I continued to help the team and didn't complain," he said. "Once you accept that you aren't an everyday player, you become better at your role."

Role player or not, Hutton had a .700 lifetime average against Tom Seaver and became a fine pinch hitter. His best season was 1977, when he hit .309 for the Phillies in 107 games.

PHILADELPHIA PHILLIES

TOMMY
HUTTON

INFIELD

Photo provided by author

#14 TOMMY HUTTON • INFIELD
Phillies, Dodgers, Expos, Blue Jays

Born: 4/20/1946 Los Angeles CA
Height: 5-11 • Weight: 180 lbs. • Bats left • Throws left
12 year Major League Career • .248 avg. • 22 HR • 186 RBI
Phillies 6 years • Major League Debut: 1966

His memories of Philadelphia and his six years with the Phillies are good ones.

"I came up in the Dodgers organization and was a West Coast guy who didn't know that much about the East Coast," Hutton said. "In '72 we weren't a very good team. But they were building and looking to the future, trying to get better. Paul Owens replaced Frank Lucchesi as manager to find out who could play.

"The atmosphere was fun, and the fans were always into the game. You always knew what they wanted. I had a chance to play with some great guys like Mike Schmidt, Steve Carlton, Larry Bowa, Dave Cash, Richie Allen and Greg Luzinski. They were just great teammates."

Hutton left the Phillies prior to the 1978 season and went north of the border with the Toronto Blue Jays, where he hit .254 before being sent to Montreal that same year. He spent four years in Montreal before his playing days ended in 1981.

Tommy Hutton then began what has been a very successful career as a broadcaster. A 40-year veteran of the game, Hutton only had two days off between his playing and broadcasting careers. After being released by the Expos on a Sunday, he joined their broadcasting team the following Wednesday. "I've been very fortunate," said Hutton, who recently got his second World Series ring in six years as an announcer for the Florida Marlins. "I've worked with some great people and some good organizations, including ESPN."

Before working for the Marlins, Hutton also announced Yankees and Blue Jays games.

One of his sons, Jason, who was drafted by the Chicago White Sox, runs the Tommy Hutton Baseball Academy, while his other son, Derek, is a pro prospect at second base. Hutton and former teammate Dick Ruthven are brothers-in-law.

"I'd just like the fans to remember me as a guy who played hard and accepted his role," he said.

NIPPY JONES

Vernal "Nippy" Jones had a modest major league career, enjoying his most successful campaign with St. Louis in 1949, hitting .300 with eight home runs and 62 RBIs in 110 games. That followed up a strong season in 1948 in which he hit a respectable .254 with 10 homers and 81 RBIs, both career highs, in 132 games.

But back problems limited his playing time, and he never played regularly again. Jones did appear in 80 games for the '51 Cards, hitting .263 before coming to the Phillies the following year, where he appeared in just eight games.

Jones disappeared from the major leagues for five seasons until he resurfaced with Milwaukee in 1957 at the age of 32 after playing for Sacramento of the Pacific Coast League in early July. He did see action in 30 games during the remainder of the season, but will forever be remembered for his postseason at-bat in the 1957 World Series against the New York Yankees. He went hitless, didn't score and never played on the field. But it was his quick thinking in the famous shoe black incident that helped the Braves defeat the heavily favored Yanks.

With his team trailing the Yankees, 5-4, in the bottom of the 10th inning of Game 4, Jones was sent up to pinch hit for pitcher

nippy jones

PHILLIES INFIELD

#9 NIPPY JONES • INFIELD
Phillies, Cardinals, Brewers

Born: 6/29/1925 Los Angeles CA • Died: 10/3/1995 Sacramento CA
Height: 5-11 • Weight: 180 lbs. • Bats left • Throws left
8 year Major League Career • .267 avg. • 25 HR • 209 RBI
Phillies 1 year • Major League Debut: 1946

Warren Spahn. New York pitcher Tommy Bryne threw a pitch that hit Jones on the shoe, but the umpire, Augie Donatelli, thought it was a ball in the dirt.

"Byrne started me off with a curveball," Jones said in an interview years later. "The ball hit me on the foot and I dropped my bat and started toward first base. But Augie Donatelli said, 'Come back here. That's ball one.' I couldn't believe it. I went right for the ball and Yogi Berra was pretty smart, so he did the same thing. I got there first, and there was a spot of shoe polish about a half-inch in diameter."

After he retrieved the ball, Jones showed it to Donatelli, who saw the shoe polish smudge and awarded him first base. Felix Mantilla came in to pinch run for Jones. Johnny Logan doubled Mantilla home to tie the score before Eddie Mathews cracked a game-winning home run off Bob Grim to win the game for the Braves and tie the series at two games each.

Lew Burdette later shut out the Yankees, 5-0, in Game 7 to capture the championship for Milwaukee.

Less than a week after the World Series ended, the Braves sent Jones to Wichita in the American Association. He refused to report, was released and returned to the Pacific Coast League, where he played until the end of the 1960 season. He never played in another major league game.

LEN MATUSZEK

This product of the Phillies' farm system had some power, but never really got much of an opportunity to show what he could do as an everyday player. He replaced Pete Rose as the Phillies' everyday first-sacker in September of 1983 and helped the team drive to the playoffs, hitting .275 with four home runs and 16 RBIs. But he was left off of the postseason roster.

"I'm still very proud of what I did during September of '83 when I took over for Pete," Matuszek said from his Cincinnati home. "You feel pressure to play well in Philadelphia. We went on something like a 10-game winning streak, and I was right in the middle of it. And Pete was on the bench for the first time in his career."

Matuszek played most of the '84 season as the team's first baseman and responded with a .248 average with 12 home runs, although he admitted that he was trying too hard, as if he could hit a five-run homer every time up. Drafted by the Phillies in the fifth round of the draft, he got some chances. But his Midwestern approach may not have been what the team had in mind long term.

"From an organizational standpoint, the Phillies drafted me and game me a shot, but I always kind of felt that they just didn't think I was one of their guys," Matuszek said. "I'm a laid back Midwesterner,

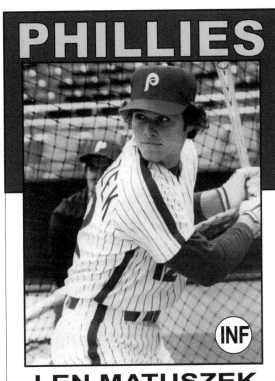

PHILLIES

INF

LEN MATUSZEK

Photo provided by author

#24 LEN MATUSZEK • INFIELD

Phillies, Blue Jays, Dodgers

Born: 9/27/1954 Toledo OH
Height: 6-2 • Weight: 195 lbs. • Bats left • Throws right
7 year Major League Career • .234 avg. • 30 HR • 119 RBI
Phillies 4 years • Major League Debut: 1981

which is different from a Philadelphia person. The people were so ravenous for success. I was lucky enough to come in and get pinch hits in three of my first four at-bats. The fans and the media were always good to me. I just felt a little bit on the outside. You always look back and wonder.

"Mike Schmidt struggled with the fans, but he had the same thoughts that I did. You go out and do your job and not show any emotion on your sleeve."

Matuszek was sent to Toronto and finally the Dodgers, where he became a valuable player who proved once more to be a dependable pinch hitter.

He hit .261 for LA in 1986 with nine homers, but was gone in 1987 after a series of injuries limited his effectiveness. On June 1, 1984, Matuszek became the 18th player in major league history to play an entire game at first base without a single putout in a 12-3 loss to the Cubs.

Following his playing career, Matuszek became a sports reporter and anchor in Cincinnati and then worked in the financial service industry. Still involved with baseball academies and coaching, he became a primary caregiver. His new career is rewarding and gratifying, but he looks back to his days in Philadelphia with pride and fondness.

"I was proud to wear the Phillies uniform," he said. "I would like to be remembered as someone who took the game seriously, who wanted to win and gave an honest effort. There was not a time when I did not prepare myself. I wanted to win and to be a part of winning."

One of his sons, Kyle, plays baseball at West Virginia University, and his other son, Kevin, plays professionally in an independent league.

PETE ROSE

Did Pete Rose bet on baseball?

Yes.

Does he belong in the Hall of Fame?

That depends on who you talk to.

Without a doubt, Pete Rose put up the numbers to be elected to baseball's hallowed hall. A lifetime .303 hitter, he hit at least .301 a total of 15 times en route to becoming baseball's all-time hit leader with 4,256.

Not as widely known, Rose is also the career leader in at-bats with 14,053, singles with 3,215, and games played with 3,562. In addition, Rose averaged 1.19 hits per game, an amazing statistic. In his 24-year major league career, he led the league in hitting three times, was first in hits seven times, and also topped the 200 hit mark 10 times.

Everyone remembers how Pete Rose would bust it down the line to first base, even after he would draw a walk from the opposing pitcher. But he also stole 198 bases.

Putting runs on the board is vital to team success. Pete Rose drove in 1,314 runs and scored another 2,165. So he had a hand in 3,479 runs in 3,562 games.

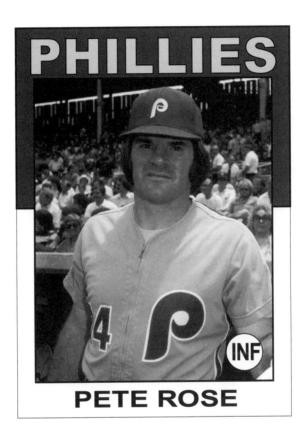

PHILLIES

PETE ROSE

#14 PETE ROSE • INFIELD
Phillies, Reds, Expos

Born: 4/14/1941 Cincinnati OH
Height: 5-11 • Weight: 200 lbs. • Bats both • Throws right
24 year Major League Career • .303 avg. • 160 HR • 1314 RBI
Phillies 5 years • Major League Debut: 1963

Certainly Hall of Fame credentials. But...

In an agreement with the late baseball commissioner Bart Giamatti in 1989, Rose accepted a lifetime suspension with no chance to come back to the game or gain entrance to the Hall of Fame. In that agreement he did not admit gambling on baseball. Now, 14 years later, No. 14 has admitted that he did in fact bet on baseball numerous times during his tenure as Cincinnati Reds manager in his bestselling book, *My Prison Without Bars.*

Ever since the dark days of 1919 and the Black Sox scandal in Chicago, gambling on baseball has been taboo for players, coaches and managers. You just don't do it. Rose knew the rule and flagrantly broke it.

It's unfortunate that his lifetime suspension overshadowed so many marvelous accomplishments during his playing career. Prior to his suspension, Rose managed the Reds to a 412-373 record in six seasons.

Nicknamed Charlie Hustle for his endless enthusiasm by Yankees great Whitey Ford, this Cincinnati native took the game to a new level. He was a catalyst for the Big Red Machine of the '70s and is largely credited with getting the also-ran Phillies over the top to the world championship in 1980.

"I love Pete Rose," said his former teammate Larry Christenson. "A lot of people have feelings about Pete and what he has done. When I think about Pete, I think about what a blood-and-guts player he was on the field. He was totally supportive of his teammates. If you had family or friends in the clubhouse, Pete would come over and talk to them and basically make a fuss. He was a very generous person, a great friend, teammate and a special player.

"I think he should be in the Hall of Fame, absolutely."

His competitive drive has never been questioned by those who saw him bowl over Oakland catcher Ray Fosse in the 12th inning of the 1970 All-Star Game. His fight with New York Mets shortstop Bud Harrelson in Game 3 of the LCS against the New York Mets prompted a bench-clearing brawl.

"He deserves to be in the Hall of Fame," said former Phillies pitcher Larry Colton, who gave up one of Rose's 4.256 hits. "If they are so worried about the integrity of the game, they should do something about the use of steroids. That has had much more of an effect on the game than anything bad that Rose did. It's ridiculous."

As a person, Pete Rose was far from perfect. But many baseball fans consider Pete Rose the player as close to perfection as anything they've ever seen.

MIKE
SCHMIDT

After suffering through a rookie year in which he hit just .196, Michael Jack Schmidt became what most experts consider the best third baseman in the history of baseball. He led the National League in home runs eight times and in RBIs three times. A true superstar, Schmidt overcame high strikeout numbers early in his career and was inducted into the Hall of Fame in 1996 along with long-time Phillies player and broadcaster Richie Ashburn.

After his abysmal rookie year, Schmidt rebounded nicely in 1974, smashing 36 home runs, driving in 116 and hitting .282. For the next three consecutive years, he hit 38 homers per year and drove in 303 runs.

One of his most memorable home runs came off of Expos reliever Stan Bahnsen in the 1980 pennant drive. Schmidt answered all of his critics that season, hitting .286 with a career-high 48 home runs and 121 RBIs, also a career high. He helped lead the Phillies to their only world championship, hitting .381 with two homers in the Fall Classic and earned the first of three Most Valuable Player Awards.

Often misunderstood by Phillies fans, as Schmidt's career continued, even those tough critics began to realize just how special No. 20 was. Michael Jack led the league in homers eight times, was the

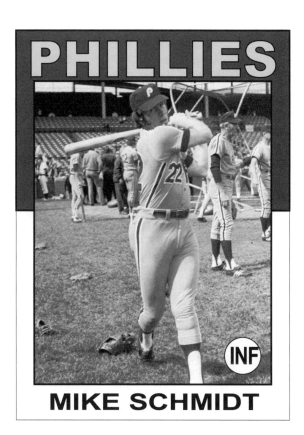

PHILLIES

MIKE SCHMIDT

#20 MIKE SCHMIDT • INFIELD
Phillies

Born: 9/27/1949 Dayton OH
Height: 6-2 • Weight: 203 lbs. • Bats right • Throws right
18 year Major League Career • .267 avg. • 548 HR • 1595 RBI
Phillies 18 years • Major League Debut: 1972

top RBI man three times and was an All-Star 11 times. Simply put, Mike Schmidt was the best.

"Mike was a great guy," said his teammate Gene Garber. "He was a good friend and one of the greatest players ever. He used to frustrate me and I'd tell him to stop thinking sometimes. But that was part of his nature. He wanted to be as good as he could possibly be. I was fortunate enough to play with some really great players and Mike was right there."

His dedication to the game and work ethic have never been questioned.

"His work habits were unbelievable," said Greg Harris, a pitcher with the Phillies in 1988 and '89. "Just the way he went about his day-to-day activity. It was really enjoyable to play with a superstar. He was quiet, but he loved to talk about baseball, like an old-school player. I enjoyed talking baseball with Mike. He has routine, so you left him alone. But he was approachable. When he was struggling, he was always open to discussing ways out of it."

Schmidt maintained his high level of play through the 1987 season in which he hit .293 with 35 homers and 113 RBIs. But he missed part of the 1988 season with a shoulder problem, limiting him to 108 games.

After a quick start the following season, with his average hovering near .200 and noticing a decline in his outstanding defensive play that earned him 10 Gold Glove Awards, Mike Schmidt announced his retirement in May of 1989. His tearful good bye from the game showed the baseball world just how much he loved the game of baseball.

He became only the 31st player to be elected to the Hall of Fame in his first year of eligibility with 96.5 percent of the vote.

Following baseball, Schmidt tried to become a professional golfer. He then began to get involved with the Phillies in spring training as an instructor as well as numerous times during recent seasons.

In October 2003, Mike Schmidt was named manager of the Phillies' farm club, The Threshers, in Clearwater, Florida.

COSTEN SHOCKLEY

John Costen Shockley was a highly touted first baseman who put up some big minor league numbers with the Arkansas Travelers prior to his recall by the Phillies in 1964, belting 36 home runs and driving in 112 runs. That powerful Little Rock team was known as the "Boom Boom Travelers," a heavy-hitting team with the likes of Shockley at first base, Norm Gigon as second, Wayne Graham at third, Pat Corrales behind the plate and an outfield of Adolfo Phillips, Alex Johnson and Bill Sorrell.

When Shockley was recalled by the Phillies in 1964, it was thought to be the start of a long major league career.

"The first time I came to bat in Philadelphia, I was booed by the fans," he said. "My first time up! They didn't know me from Adam."

He hit .229 in 11 games for the Phillies and was then dealt to the Los Angeles Angels since Dick Stuart was acquired by Philadelphia to play first base. But much like Gene Mauch, Angels skipper Bill Rigney was a manager who believed in platooning his players. As a result, Shockley got little chance to play, batting just .197 with a pair of home runs in 40 games.

Photo provided by author

#31 COSTEN SHOCKLEY • INFIELD
Phillies, Angels

Born: 2/8/1942 Georgetown DE
Height: 6-2 • Weight: 200 lbs. • Bats left • Throws left
2 year Major League Career • .197 avg. • 3 HR • 19 RBI
Phillies 1 year • Major League Debut: 1964

Blessed with great athletic ability, Costen never played regularly in the Show, and rather than report to the minor leagues again, he opted to quit the game and went to work for IA Construction Co. He was one of those prospects that seemingly should have had a long major league career.

"The Phillies traded me to the Angels and I went to spring training, and then they wanted to send me down early on," he said. "So I got involved in construction and had a great career there."

But those who saw him play thought he would have a great major league baseball career. Shockley had all of the tools and a great attitude as well.

"He was one of my teammates on the 'Boom Boom Travelers,'" said Wayne Graham, who went on to become a very successful college baseball coach at Rice University. "Costen was the best minor league player I ever saw that didn't make it in the majors. He was quite an athlete. He hit 30-some home runs in '64, he could run, he could field and he could throw. He was a great player with a great body to play the game. To me, he should have been a major league star."

After giving up the game, Shockley returned to his native Delaware and began a new life. His career in construction flourished, and he was also able to maintain some contact with baseball by coaching a Little League team to the 1980 Senior League World Championship.

Were there ever second thoughts?

"For a while I wondered if I did the right thing by retiring so early," he admitted. "But I had started a family and told myself I would not regret it or second-guess my decision. I made a good career in construction."

Shockley has two sons and five grandchildren and lives in Delaware.

FRANK THOMAS

This veteran slugger, who smacked at least 10 homers in 13 seasons, including 34 with the '62 Mets, was dealt to the Phillies in exchange for pitcher Gary Kroll and outfielder Wayne Graham on August 7, 1964. The impact of that deal was immediately felt as Frank Thomas instilled new life into the team, hitting nearly .300 with seven home runs and 26 RBIs in 39 games. But the Phillies' pennant hopes took what many thought was a fatal turn when Thomas fractured his right thumb sliding back into second base in a 3-2 loss to the Dodgers on September 8. The Phils were still six games ahead in the National League standings, but his injury was clearly the beginning of the end.

"People always say that Gene Mauch pushed the panic button by pitching Jim Bunning and Chris Short with three days' rest since he had Art Mahaffey, Ray Culp and Dennis Bennett on the team," Thomas said. "But not too long ago I was at an event with Gene, and he pointed to me and my injury when someone asked him what happened to the '64 Phillies. I was playing very well and hitting some homers, driving in a lot of runs. The team had begun to falter a little bit, but after I got hurt, it went downhill fast."

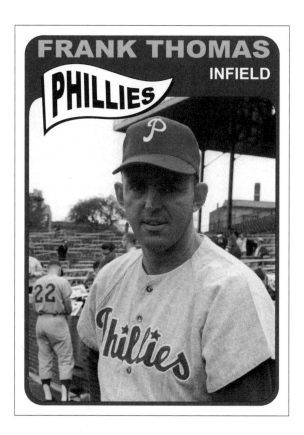

#45 FRANK THOMAS • INFIELD
Phillies, Pirates, Reds, Braves, Cubs, Astros, Mets

Born: 6/11/1929 Pittsburgh PA
Height: 6-3 • Weight: 205 lbs. • Bats right • Throws right
16 year Major League Career • .266 avg. • 286 HR • 962 RBI
Phillies 2 years • Major League Debut: 1951

Frank Thomas broke into the major leagues with a bang in his first full season in 1953, smacking 30 home runs and driving in 102, while hitting .255. He followed with at least 23 homers for each of the next five seasons, including a career-high 35 in 1958 with 109 RBIs.

When he wasn't hitting homers and driving in runs, this powerful outfielder-first baseman would bet all comers that he could catch their hardest throw barehanded and reportedly never lost any of those bets.

Thomas continued to be a valuable player with the Reds, Cubs and Braves before leading the expansion New York Mets with 34 homers, 94 RBIs and a .266 average in 1962.

After the Phillies' near-miss in 1964, Thomas was placed on waivers by the club after a confrontation with Dick Allen. Ironically, Thomas hit a pinch-hit home run to win his final game with the Phillies.

He played with the Astros and Braves as well in 1965 before finishing up with the Cubs in 1966.

After baseball, Thomas worked for the ICM School of Business until his retirement in 1984. The friendly and engaging former ballplayer still lives in his native Pittsburgh and enjoys making baseball-related appearances.

EDDIE WAITKUS

Eddie Waitkus was a line drive-hitting, outstanding-fielding first baseman who unfortunately will always be better known as the real-life Roy Hobbs character from the movie *The Natural*. On the evening of June 14, 1949, while hitting a lofty .306, Waitkus was lured to the hotel room of a woman he had never met, a 19-year-old Chicago native, Ruth Steinhagen, who had a tragic crush on Waitkus from his playing days with the Cubs. Upon his entering her room, she brought a .22 caliber rifle out of the closet and shot him in the stomach. The girl then no doubt saved his life by calling the switchboard operator to say that she had just shot a man.

Waitkus was seriously injured and near death with a bullet lodged close to his spine. He gradually improved but needed four operations to bring him back to health. He returned to again become a fine ballplayer, but was never quite the same. He hit .284 in 1950 and .289 in 1952. Eddie married one of the nurses who cared for him in the hospital, was sold to Baltimore and returned to the Phillies for his final season in 1955.

"He made a tremendous comeback after being shot," said his former teammate, pitcher Steve Ridzik. "He got married shortly after all that happened and had a baby. He and his wife were great people,

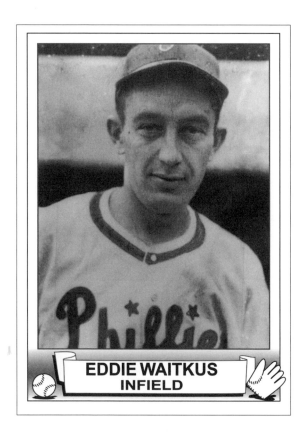

EDDIE WAITKUS
INFIELD

#4 EDDIE WAITKUS • INFIELD

Phillies, Cubs, Orioles

Born: 9/4/1919 Cambridge MA • Died: 9/15/72 Jamaica Plain MA
Height: 6-1 • Weight: 175 lbs. • Bats left • Throws left
11 year Major League Career • .285 avg. • 24 HR • 373 RBI
Phillies 6 years • Major League Debut: 1941

but Eddie had lots of problems after that happened to him. He was a great guy. You'll never hear anyone say a bad word about Eddie Waitkus."

Waitkus was traded by the Chicago Cubs to the Phillies on December 14, 1948, in exchange for Monk Dubiel and Dutch Leaonard. He was purchased by the Baltimore Orioles on March 16, 1954.

Waitkus worked as a floor manager in a Waltham, Massachusetts, department store until his death in 1972. The woman who shot him was found incapable of standing trial, spent three years in a mental institution and was released.

DAVE
WATKINS

Much like Archibald "Moonlight" Graham, the New York Giants ballplayer immortalized in the movie *Field of Dreams*, Dave Watkins had a tough decision to make after playing his rookie season with the Phillies in 1969. Should he come back and fight for a spot on the '70 roster, or return to college and follow his other dream of becoming a doctor?

Today, Dr. Dave Watkins is medical director of Frazier Rehabilitation Institute in his native Kentucky.

"It was just a good experience to get there," Watkins said of his one year in the majors. "I gave myself a few years to see what I could do. I was 26 at the time and had a taste. But at that time the money wasn't great and you needed to set yourself up, or else you'd be selling cars or insurance. So I went back to school."

Watkins specializes in physical medicine and rehabilitation and has worked with stroke victims and those with spinal cord and head injuries. He never lost his love for baseball, but he had to decide the best future for he and his family.

"I don't regret my decision," he said.

"I loved playing baseball and being around all of the players. My old coach Andy Seminick infused that attitude in me. You get

Photo provided by author

#2 DAVE WATKINS • INFIELD
Phillies

Born: 3/15/1944 Owensboro KY
Height: 5-10 • Weight: 185 lbs. • Bats right • Throws right
1 year Major League Career • .176 avg. • 4 HR • 12 RBI
Phillies 1 year • Major League Debut: 1969

ready every day, enjoy it, show up and be ready to play. I lived and breathed baseball, but I had other talents and directions as well. You have to leave yourself options for the future."

While his future took him away from baseball, he is left with fond memories of the experience and his single season in Philadelphia.

"The city itself is all about the history of America," he said. "You step back in time. I loved the place. The fans were a little fickle, but I always got along with them because I always played hard and they knew it. Connie Mack Stadium was wonderful. It was a fun park to play in."

Would Watkins have returned to the major leagues had he not quit and gone on to college? The following season, catchers Tim McCarver and Mike Ryan both broke their hands in the same inning of the same game. So the odds are that Watkins would have continued his major league career. But considering all that he has done for so many patients over the years, you get the feeling that Dr. Dave Watkins made the correct decision.

Chapter 3

OUTFIELDERS

RICHIE ASHBURN

Richie Ashburn was a part of the Phillies' baseball family for 49 years, first as an exciting center fielder and then as a broadcaster. He won over two generations of Philadelphia fans. As a player, the two-time National League batting champion also finished second to Stan Musial twice. He led the league in on-base percentage, singles and walks four times each. The fleet-footed center fielder covered lots of territory in the outfield and was an outstanding base stealer.

Whitey Ashburn was one of the stars on the 1950 Whiz Kids team that played in the World Series against the Yankees. He hit .303 with a league-leading 14 triples. He later won the batting title with a .338 average in 1955 and .350 in 1958.

"Richie kept the '50 Whiz Kids team alive," said his former teammate Putsy Caballero. "He would always write about them in the paper and talk about them during his broadcasts. He was my roommate. I named my oldest boy after Richie. He was the best ambassador that Philadelphia baseball ever had."

Ashburn was a local folk hero as a broadcaster when his second career began in 1963. He combined his astute knowledge of the game along with his droll sense of humor and Midwestern charm. Legions

#1 RICHIE ASHBURN • OUTFIELD
Phillies, Cubs, Mets

Born: 3/19/1927 Tilden NE • Died: 9/9/1997 New York NY
Height: 5-10 • Weight: 170 lbs. • Bats left • Throws right
15 year Major League Career • .308 avg. • 29 HR • 586 RBI
Phillies 11 years • Major League Debut: 1948

of fans copied his favorite sayings like, "Oh brother," "Mind like a steel trap," "He looks a little runnerish," and "Froze 'em."

Millions of Ashburn fans were thrilled that this six-time All Star was elected to the Hall of Fame by the Veterans Committee. It was felt that because of so many other great outfielders of his era, Whitey's accomplishments were overlooked. That ended when he and Mike Schmidt were both inducted in the Hall in 1995.

He and his close friend Harry Kalas were a great tandem in the announcing booth for years until Ashburn's untimely death after broadcasting a Phillies-Mets game in 1997. His loss was felt throughout the Delaware Valley and all of baseball.

Richie Ashburn was a Hall of Famer in Philadelphia long before he was enshrined in Cooperstown.

Ashburn was signed as an amateur free agent by the Phillies prior to the 1945 season. On January 11, 1960, he was traded to the Chicago Cubs for John Buzhardt, Alvin Dark and Jim Woods.

RICK BOSETTI

To say that Rick Bosetti was quite a character is a huge understatement. Bo broke in to the majors with the '76 Phillies hitting a respectable .276 in 13 games. He was a player who wore his heart on his sleeve, and the faithful in the stands liked what they saw of this exuberant young player. Those Philadelphia squads of the mid- to late '70s were loaded with talent, making it difficult for a young player to break into the lineup.

"I had come up through the Phillies organization, and I loved it," Bosetti said. "I came from a blue-collar background, and you really appreciate special things that happen to you. Even though I was there for a short time, the fans were very accommodating of me and I related to them. They saw that I really worked hard. Everybody in the stands thinks that they could play in the major leagues because everyone played baseball. I think I kind of acted like most of them would have acted if they were given the chance."

Bosetti was sent to St. Louis, where he played in just 41 games in 1977. His baseball career seemed to be on the way up with a trade to Toronto, where he played regularly for two years, in March of 1978 in exchange for Tom Bruno.

PHILADELPHIA PHILLIES

RICK
BOSETTI

OUTFIELD

#29, 28 RICK BOSETTI • OUTFIELD

Phillies, Cards, Blue Jays, A's

Born: 8/5/1953 Redding CA
Height: 5-11 • Weight: 185 lbs. • Bats right • Throws right
7 year Major League Career • .250 avg. • 17 HR • 133 RBI
Phillies 1 year • Major League Debut: 1976

With the Blue Jays, Bosetti became the regular center fielder, hitting .259 in 1978 and .260 the following year, playing in all 162 games.

But his broke his arm early in the 1980 season and never got the chance to play regularly again, as a young outfielder named Lloyd Moseby made the most of his opportunity with the Blue Jays.

"I was the kind of player who needed to play every day to be a benefit to the team," Bosetti said. "It takes a special type of player to come off the bench. I was the kind of player that needed to know that they had confidence in me and that I'd continue to get a chance to play."

After being relegated to a backup role, he played out the string until 1982 when he finished up in six games for Oakland. But when he played regularly, Bo was the type of player who could hit .260 and was an outstanding outfielder.

An interesting kind of guy, Bosetti was able to literally leave his mark on nearly every major league outfield. Once before a Triple-A game in Oklahoma City, he relieved himself in the outfield since the players' facilities were far away. He continued and expanded his trademark hobby in the majors, urinating in the outfield of every American League stadium and a majority of National League parks, which must be a record of some sort.

"All the publicity started when Rick Cerone mentioned me in a magazine article about flakes of the game," Bosetti said. "It got blown all out of proportion and people would watch to see if they could catch me. I never did it during a game. Hey, I was 24 years old and it was all in fun."

Following his baseball career, Rick got involved in the technology field and purchased a company called Team Solutions, with locations in Chico, Eureka, and his hometown of Redding, California. He has also been very involved in his community, coaching baseball and swimming. A member of the Planning Commission in Shasta County, he is a candidate for the Board of Supervisors.

Bosetti loved his time with the Phillies organization.

"I just hope that people will remember me as someone who gave everything he had when he was on the field," he said. "That's the way I played the game. I was nuts, but I played hard."

JOHNNY CALLISON

This strong-armed right fielder was a solid performer for the Phillies during the 1960s, hitting more than 30 home runs and driving in over 100 runs two times. He was the hero of the 1964 All-Star team when he led the National League to victory with a three-run blast off Dick Radatz at Shea Stadium.

Johnny Callison came to the Phillies after two brief stints with the Chicago White Sox in exchange for Gene Freese. The young outfielder responded by becoming a premier outfielder. He hit 112 home runs over a four-year period from 1962 to 1965. He belted 31 in '64 and 32 in '65.

On November 17, 1969, he was traded to the Chicago Cubs in exchange for Dick Selma and Oscar Gamble.

This fine fielder with a shotgun arm from right field also led the league in triples twice and in doubles once. He was an immensely popular player who is still a fan favorite.

"My memories of playing in Philadelphia are pretty good ones," Callison said. "I enjoyed playing there. I was there for 10 years. If you play hard, the fans are behind you. If you slough off, they'll boo you. I played hard and gave 100 percent, and they knew I did. They were very good to me."

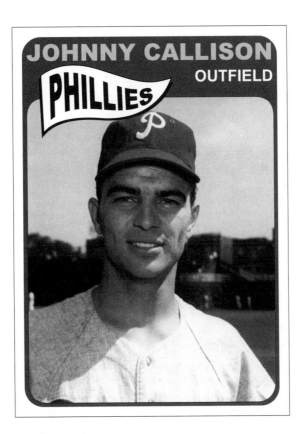

#6 JOHNNY CALLISON • OUTFIELD
Phillies, White Sox, Cubs, Yankees

Born: 3/12/1939 Qualls OK
Height: 5-10 • Weight: 175 lbs. • Bats left • Throws right
16 year Major League Career • .264 avg. • 226 HR • 840 RBI
Phillies 10 years • Major League Debut: 1958

After a 10-year tenure in Philadelphia, Callison was dealt to the Chicago Cubs for a young outfielder named Oscar Gamble. He had a solid 1970 in Wrigley Field, hitting .264 with 19 home runs and 68 RBIs. After slumping the following season, he spent the final two years of his career coming off the bench with the New York Yankees, finishing up in 1973.

"Johnny and I are close friends," said former teammate Doug Clemens. "He was a great Phillies baseball player. He had the fastest release in the outfield that I ever saw. He was a great outfielder and a damn good hitter."

Johnny Callison will always be remembered as a clutch ballplayer who almost led the team to the pennant in 1964. He was a key player for the team that had a magical summer, right up until the last couple of weeks of the season. The collapse of that Phillies team will never be forgotten.

"I think we just ran out of gas," he said. "We played so hard all year long and just ran out. Things went right all year. When things were going good, more good things follow. We saw that for most of the season. But when it starts to go bad, things seem to go against you and you can't stop it. It was nobody's fault. We won an awful lot of games in the eighth inning that year. Then it stopped. And then the bullpen started to go bad."

Part of Callison's popularity probably came from the fact that he was thought of as an average guy who was a great ballplayer. Even after his playing days ended, he continued to be just one of us.

"I compare Johnny to a guy who came up with Boston when I was pitching there, Dwight Evans," said former Phillies pitcher Ray Culp. "They were both so good defensively. The runners didn't take an extra base on either one of them ever. They were both good hitters, but I think of defense when I think of them. They just never made a bad play and really knew the game."

In 1991, John Callison wrote a book chronicling his career, *The Johnny Callison Story.*

"After my career ended, I worked as a car salesman and bartender for a while," said Callison, who still lives in the Philadelphia suburbs. "Now I'm retired."

DOUG CLEMENS

This former football player at Syracuse University saw his gridiron career cut short by a knee injury, which enabled him to put all of his emphasis on baseball. In fact, the University switched his scholarship from football to baseball. Growing up in Leesport, Pennsylvania, near Reading, Doug Clemens was a Phillies fan as a kid.

"I was always a Phillies fan," he said. "My father was a bird dog for the Phillies and my high school coach. He coached everything and he had the record for the most victories of all coaches in the state of Pennsylvania."

After being signed by St. Louis prior to the 1960 season, Clemens was sent to Billings in the Pioneer League, where he tore up the place, hitting .389 in 39 games.

He spent parts of the next four years up and down with the Cardinals, hitting well in the minors but getting little opportunity to play regularly in the Show. His best time in St. Louis was 1962, when he hit .237 in 48 games.

Clemens was part of one of baseball's biggest trades, as he was dealt from the Cards, along with pitchers Ernie Brojlio and Bobby Schantz, to the Chicago Cubs in exchange for Lou Brock, Jack Spring and Paul Toth. After the trade, Clemens had his one chance to play as

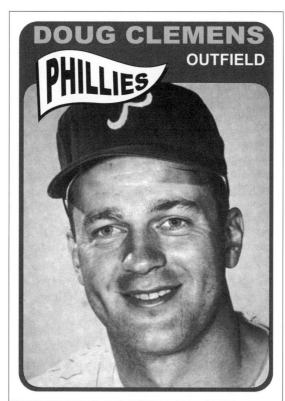

Photo © The Phillies

#17 DOUG CLEMENS • OUTFIELD

Cards, Cubs, Phillies

Born: 6/9/1939 Leesport PA
Height: 6-0 • Weight: 180 lbs. • Bats left • Throws right
9 year Major League Career • .229 avg. • 12 HR • 88 RBI
Phillies 3 years • Major League Debut: 1960

a regular with the Cubs. In 1965, Clemens hit over .400 in spring and had his busiest big-league season, appearing in 128 games, but he hit just .221.

"To be honest, the Cubs gave me a great opportunity in 1965," he said. "It was my best opportunity to play on a regular basis. I wish the results were better. I just did not produce. The pitchers at the major league level have better control, regardless of what the count is. They nibble and get pitches that may be a little off the plate. They get to know you and determine what your weaknesses might be. I just wasn't getting the hits. But I did the best I could.

"I had good minor league credentials. But the higher you go the tougher it gets. In retrospect, I should have done better. I was fast and had a good bat."

The following January, he was dealt to the Phillies in exchange for Wes Covington. After playing for Leo Durocher in Chicago, Clemens then played for Gene Mauch with the Phillies.

"Gene Mauch I would rate as the best major league manager in baseball at that time," he said. "He was a great strategist who really knew the game. He was a scrappy, take-no-prisoners type of guy."

In 1966, his first year in Philadelphia, Clemens had his best career big-league average of .256. He could play all three outfield positions and was an outstanding pinch hitter. In fact, the following season, Clemens tied a major league record by hitting three pinch-hit doubles in three consecutive games.

He retired after the 1968 season after qualifying for the major league pension. A great opportunity presented itself out of baseball, but with expansion and two new teams coming into the league, he might have gotten another chance to play regularly again. Did Doug Clemens quit too soon?

"In retrospect, yes," he said. "At the same time, I had five knee operations. Playing every day takes a toll on your legs. I would have enjoyed playing more. Of course, there is no guarantee I would have been picked by one of the expansion clubs. But a good friend of mine in Bucks County asked me to come and work for him. It has been a great situation."

Clemens is now the vice president of sales and marketing for General Machine Products, in suburban Philadelphia. While he has thrived in the business world, he still looks back with great fondness on his days as a major league baseball player.

"I have no regrets when I look back on it," he said. "I'm very pleased with the career I had. It was important for me and it was great for raising kids. Baseball is a wonderful extension of my life.

"I'd like to be remembered as someone who gave it his best shot, who tried to excel for the benefit of the team and himself. I used to preach that there are five things that make up a good ballplayer: running, fielding, throwing, hitting and hitting for power. There is a sixth that is an intangible: attitude. Whatever I lacked in the first five I compensated for with a good attitude."

WAYNE GRAHAM

Those who can, do; those that can't, teach. That old saying may have been made with Wayne Graham in mind. This third baseman-outfielder was only able to muster seven hits in 55 big-league at-bats. But he was an outstanding minor league player, hitting .300 or more six times in his career. He was the Texas minor league Player of the Year when he hit .311 with 17 home runs and 70 RBIs for Dallas-Fort Worth in 1962.

Graham was signed by the Phillies as an amateur free agent prior to the 1957 season. On August 7, 1964, he was traded by the Phillies with Gary Kroll and cash to the New York Mets in exchange for Frank Thomas. The Mets, on February 22, 1966, traded Graham, Bobby Klaus and Jimmie Schaffer to the Phillies in exchange for Dick Stuart.

Along the way, he was part of the powerful 1964 "Boom Boom Travelers," the Phillies' Triple A affiliate in Little Rock. He made the most of his two brief encounters in the major leagues, playing under Gene Mauch with the '63 Phillies and legendary Casey Stengel with the '64 Mets.

In an odd way, Graham helped keep the Phillies' pennant hopes alive when he was traded to New York in the summer of 1964 along

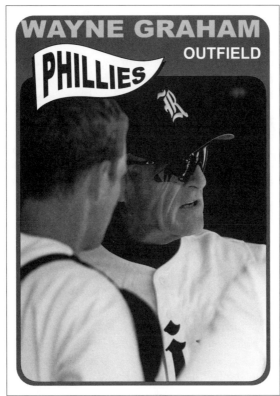

Photo provided by Rice University Athletic Dept.

#34 WAYNE GRAHAM • OUTFIELD
Phillies, Mets

Born: 4/8/1937 Yoakum TX
Height: 6-0 • Weight: 200 lbs. • Bats right • Throws right
2 year Major League Career • .127 avg. • 0 HR • 0 RBI
Phillies 1 year • Major League Debut: 1963

with pitcher Gary Kroll in exchange for slugger Frank Thomas, who nearly led the Phillies to the pennant. Thomas ignited the Phillies offense until breaking his thumb.

"It was a different world in those days," Graham said. "Most players weren't making much money. In '63, I was coming off two All-Star seasons and hoped I would get a chance with the Phillies at third base. Then they got Don Hoak to play third, and I was sent down because Tony Taylor got hurt in a game. As a result they kept Cookie Rojas instead of me. Then I got traded to the Mets, where I didn't do well at all. But I got to listen to Casey Stengel, who was great. Playing for Mauch and Stengel probably meant a lot to my success as a coach."

After his 11-year playing career ended, Wayne Graham returned to school and earned his B.S. in physical education from the University of Texas in 1970 and a master's of education in 1973 from the University of Houston.

He began his coaching career at Scarborough High School in Houston, and in 10 years on the high school level, his teams compiled a 98-13 record, with seven district titles. Right from the beginning, Graham knew he found his place as a coach.

"I was so focused on playing during my career that the idea of being a manager or coach happened by default," he said. "My desire to stay in the game brought me to coaching. The day I walked on the field as a coach, I never had a doubt that I'd be successful. It's what I was born to do.

"I had no doubt I would be successful; I know the game. But there is also true baseball logic that not everyone has."

Graham then moved on to San Jacinto-North Junior College and led the Gators to five national championships in six years, including three straight national titles. Two of his pitchers were Roger Clemens and Andy Pettitte.

He has been the head baseball coach at Rice University for 11 seasons and boasts one of the best programs in college baseball. Leading the Owls to three College World Series appearances in the past six seasons, Graham has the best coaching percentage in Rice history at .695 and has won championships for seven consecutive seasons, including the 2002 WAC title. He was named National Coach of the Year by Collegiate Baseball and led Rice to its first national championship in any sport in 2003.

Graham has had 29 consecutive winning seasons at the high school and collegiate levels, winning nearly 80 percent of his games at the collegiate level, with a 1,052-321 record at San Jacito and Rice.

In addition to Clemens and Pettitte, former Wayne Graham players in the majors also include Jose Cruz Jr., Matt Anderson and Lance Berkman.

"Gene Mauch was the great strategist, and Casey Stengel knew how to deal with the players and the media," Graham said. "He also had a great knowledge of pitching. I was raised in baseball and had a good background with 10 years of professional ball. I have a real passion for the game. I love it. I turned an addiction into a job. To be successful, you have to have a unique capacity to focus on the game and have passion for it."

DON LOCK

Don Lock was a big, strong outfielder who could hit with power. The former captain of the Wichita University basketball squad could also miss the ball, as he struck out nearly 25 percent of the time, with 776 career whiffs in 921 games.

He slugged 30 home runs in 1959 with Greensboro of the Carolina League, 35 the following season in Binghamton of the Eastern League, and 29 with Richmond of the International League in 1961. In July of 1962, the Yankees dealt Lock to the Washington Senators for Dale Long, and Lock hit a respectable .253 with 12 home runs for the Senators the rest of that season.

The following year, his first full major league season, Lock hit .252 with 27 homers and 82 RBIs. He whiffed a career-high 151 times in 149 games, but production is production. He was gaining a reputation as a feared right-handed hitter.

"I could catch the ball a little, throw it a little and hit with a lot of power," Don Lock said. "But I struck out too much. In this day and age they don't even think about that. It's a different game now. Nobody even mentions if you strike out a lot today."

In 1964, he hit a career-high 28 homers with 80 RBIs, hitting a respectable .248. But over the next two seasons, Lock suffered through

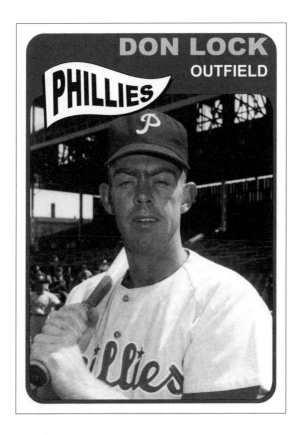

#20 DON LOCK • OUTFIELD

Phillies, Senators, Red Sox

Born: 7/27/1936 Wichita KS
Height: 6-2 • Weight: 202 lbs. • Bats right • Throws right
8 year Major League Career • .238 avg. • 122 HR • 373 RBI
Phillies 3 years • Major League Debut: 1962

a power outage that saw him hit just 16 dingers in each of those seasons, and in the winter of 1966, he was dealt to the Phillies in exchange for pitcher Darold Knowles and cash.

Lock had a respectable first year with the Phillies, hitting .252 with 14 homers and 51 RBIs. But he was platooned and really needed to play more regularly to be effective.

"I didn't do much in Philly," he said. "Gene Mauch was a platoon manager. It was his way and it was just the way he did it. When a right-hand hitter is platooned, he only faces left-hand pitching, so you wind up playing maybe one game in every series, unless you play a team with two lefties on their staff. You just don't play that much. Some guys can adjust to that, but for me it was difficult because I had a long swing."

National League pitchers began to take advantage of Lock's big swing in 1968. That coupled with less playing time resulted in a disappointing .210 average with just eight home runs in 99 games.

In May of 1969, he was sent to the Boston Red Sox in exchange for Rudy Schlessinger. He hit .224 in 53 games for the Bosox, hitting his final career home run.

"That was the twilight of a mediocre career," Lock said. "I caddied for Yaz a little bit. After that I managed in the minor leagues for the Red Sox for three years. But in those days you didn't make any money and had to do just about everything. There was just not any money to speak of and my kids were getting a little older and I wanted to spend more time with them. It was easy to quit at that point."

Lock returned to his native Kansas and became a farmer. He has fond memories of his baseball career.

"It enabled me to do what I wanted to do for a long time," he said. "It was very enjoyable and I had a lot of fun with it. I did the best I could. That's as good as it gets. I made a lot of friends in the game."

SAM PARRILLA

S am Parrilla was a hard-hitting outfielder who was originally signed by the Cleveland Indians. In his six-year career in the Tribe farm system, he hit .315, .299 and .283. But after slumping to .202 with Waterbury in 1968, he was released and signed by then Phillies farm director Paul Owens.

Parrilla responded with a .383 average in Raleigh-Durham with career highs in home runs with 28 and RBIs with 85 in 1969.

The following spring, the likable outfielder earned a spot on the Phillies' opening day roster after having a torrid spring training. Unfortunately, once the season began, the magic ended, as he saw little playing time and hit just .125 in 11 games. Hall of Famer Willie Mays robbed Parrilla of a home run by leaping over the fence at Candlestick Park to catch a ball that had the distance.

Parrilla was sent back to the minor league and later played in the Baltimore Orioles organization, but never played another game in major league baseball.

Sadly, Sam Parrilla died of an apparently self-inflicted gunshot wound. His daughter, Lana, is a popular actress who has appeared in several television series that include *Boomtown*, *JAG* and *The Shield*.

PHILADELPHIA PHILLIES

SAM
PARRILLA

OUTFIELD

#27 SAM PARRILLA • OUTFIELD
Phillies

Born: 6/12/1943 Santurce PR • Died: 2/9/1994 Brooklyn NY
Height: 5-11 • Weight: 185 lbs. • Bats right • Throws right
1 year Major League Career • .125 avg. • 0 HR • 0 RBI
Phillies 1 year • Major League Debut: 1970

BILL ROBINSON

Early in his career, Bill Robinson was heralded as the next Mickey Mantle with the New York Yankees. That's tough billing for any young player. He hit just .196 in his first full season as a Yank in 1967, but Robinson did rebound with a .240 average in 1968.

While he never came into his own in Yankee Stadium, he resurfaced with the Phillies and began to build a fine major league career out of the Yankee Stadium spotlight.

When he was called up by the Phillies in 1972, Robinson began a tradition of standing by home plate in the bullpen as Steve Carlton would warm up before games he pitched. Lefty won 27 games that year, 15 in a row with Robinson watching him throw.

"I always tried to be prepared and ready, and going down to the bullpen helped me do that," Robinson said. "I asked Steve if he minded if I stood like a batter and he said that he didn't. It gave him a chance to pitch to a hitter and gave me a chance to see some pitches. He won that first game in Montreal and then a whole lot more."

After getting his feet wet with a .239 average with eight home runs and 21 RBIs in 82 games that season, Robinson had a solid year for the Phillies in 1973, hitting a respectable .288 with 25 home runs and 65 RBIs in 124 games.

PHILADELPHIA PHILLIES

BILL
ROBINSON

OUTFIELD

#24 BILL ROBINSON • OUTFIELD

Phillies, Braves, Yankees, Pirates

Born: 6/26/1943 McKeesport PA
Height: 6-3 • Weight: 205 lbs. • Bats right • Throws right
16 year Major League Career • .258 avg. • 166 HR • 641 RBI
Phillies 5 years • Major League Debut: 1966

After one more season in Philadelphia, he had his best seasons with the Pirates in the mid-70s. With Pittsburgh, Robinson was referred to as a super-regular who didn't have a regular position. But his outstanding play and clutch hitting made him a force to be reckoned with in the powerful Pittsburgh lineup.

He hit 21 homers for the Pirates in 1976, hitting .303. What followed was his finest big-league campaign in 1977, when Robbie hit for a .304 average with 26 round-trippers and 104 RBIs, all his major league career highs.

He returned to the Phillies as a reserve in 1982 and did a respectable job off the bench. Robinson had his biggest years with the Pirates, while during his two tours of duty with the Phillies, 1973 remained his finest season.

One of the nice guys of the game, Robinson made the area his home and still lives in the South Jersey.

"I've always had a very different kind of relationship with Philly," he said. "I never had the luxury of living in the city I played until '82 with the Phillies. Even though I had a big year with the Phillies in '73, I never really established roots as a player here, or got my feet on the ground. But this area became home. Washington Township is where I decided to raise my family. We just stayed here and are all New Jerseyans now."

Following his playing career, he stayed in the game as a coach for the world champion Mets, as well as a minor league instructor for the Phillies and Yankees. Most recently, he served as a coach for the world champion Florida Marlins in 2003. He also operates the Bill Robinson Hitting Academy in South Jersey.

One of the most popular players to wear the Phillies' red and white, Bill Robinson always conducted himself like a true professional and treated everyone with respect. It was a constant, whether he was hitting .304 or .216.

"I would like to be remembered as a class individual," Robinson said. "No Hall of Fame numbers, but a good ballplayer who you could count on who was a credit to the Phillies, my race and humanity. I always tried to be the consummate professional."

MIKE ROGODZINSKI

Rogo was a popular player during his brief three-year stint with the Phillies. In his best season of 1975, this utility man and excellent pinch hitter had an average of .263. He also had an on-base percentage of .337.

Although he played in just 66 games that year, his career high, Rogodzinski had a strong following among the Phillies faithful. They liked what they saw of this left-handed hitter with a smooth swing.

"I was a hard worker, a blue-collar guy just like the fans," Rogodzinski said. "If you do well the fans treat you like royalty. If you don't, they treat you like you deserve to be treated.

"The fans are as fair as fair can be. I really appreciated and was thankful for the joy that they gave me when I did well. It made me feel so good."

A high draft choice by the organization, Rogodzinski tried to make the most of every break he got. "I was fortunate enough to be a number-two draft choice, so I always got a little extra look. Andy Seminick really gave me the opportunity to get to the big leagues. It was great. The Phillies have always treated myself and my family very well."

PHILADELPHIA PHILLIES

MIKE
ROGODZINSKI   OUTFIELD

Photo provided by author

#29 MIKE ROGODZINSKI • OUTFIELD
Phillies

Born: 2/22/1948 Evanston IL
Height: 6-0 • Weight: 185 lbs. • Bats left • Throws right
3 year Major League Career • .219 avg. • 2 HR • 12 RBI
Phillies 3 years • Major League Debut: 1973

He returned to the Phillies for 17 games the following season, but hit just .067. Given another chance in 1975, Rogodzinski responded by hitting .263 in 16 games.

Following his baseball career, he remained in the South Jersey area and has been selling retail furniture for 30 years. Initially he worked for Nate Ben's Reliable in Philadelphia and has spent quite a few years with Quality Discount Furniture in South Jersey. Still living in the Laurel Springs area, Rogo has also been involved in coaching baseball and hockey. But he still hasn't lost that baseball bug.

"I still go to the games and get frustrated like I did when I was a player," he said. "But I still love it. Baseball has been my life for so long that it's hard to get it out."

LONNIE SMITH

Lonnie Smith was an impact player with the Phillies, but was never really able to crack the starting lineup as an everyday player. He did play fairly regularly in 1980, hitting .339 in 100 games. During his long major league career, Smith hit .300 six times. He helped the Cardinals to a world championship in 1982 by leading the team in hits, doubles, triples, average, runs and steals. But his time in the Phillies organization holds fond memories.

"It was my original organization, so most of the memories of my time there are good," Lonnie Smith said. "Most people think about the '80 season, but I really enjoyed my time in the minor league system playing with guys like Dickie Noles and Kevin Saucier. After getting up to the big leagues I remember the experience in the clubhouse. You had Schmidt and Luzinski hitting all those home runs, Rose hustled all the time and did interviews day in and day out. The camaraderie of Bowa kidding in the clubhouse. When I got traded I hated it. But you adapt and go on. It was a wonderful organization with a number of good individuals."

Smith also had what he felt was a good relationship with Phillies' fans, who have a reputation for being tough on athletes. "I thought they treated me as well as could be expected," he said. "Some fans just

Photo provided by author

PHILLIES

LONNIE SMITH

OF

#27 LONNIE SMITH • OUTFIELD

Phillies, Cards, Royals, Braves

Born: 12/22/1995 Chicago IL
Height: 5-9 • Weight: 170 lbs. • Bats right • Throws right
15 year Major League Career • .289 avg. • 90 HR • 504 RBI
Phillies 4 years • Major League Debut: 1978

don't like you, and there's nothing you can do about that. But most of the people treated me fairly. When I played well, it went very well."

Lonnie Smith also overcame a drug problem later in his career that was made public after he was already clean. But FBI interviews, random drug testing, community service and a suspension followed. It was ironic that it all became public when he had already overcome his problems.

"I was two years sober before I went to the Pittsburgh cocaine trial," he said. "It was a real down in my career even though my life was really picking up."

Smith played well for the Cardinals and then was moved to Kansas City to allow more playing time for Vince Coleman and finally to Atlanta, where he continued to post good numbers. Thanks to some sound financial planning, Lonnie and his wife now raise their children together. While he would like to get back into the game someday, that is not as easy as it might seem.

"I'm still thinking about it," he said. "At this point my wife and kids enjoy me being home. But I still have desires to get back in the game. But it's hard to get back in once you're out. You have to know someone willing to give you a chance.

"I hope that the people will remember me as a player who went out and played hard and did the best he could. That's all anyone should ever want."

Chapter 4

FINAL OUTS

Since this project began in earnest, a number of members of the Phillies' family have passed away. The beloved Pope, **Paul Owens**, former farm director, scout, manager and general manager died after a long illness. As farm director, he was responsible for the signing and development of many of the players who played on the many great Phillies teams in the 1970s, culminating with the World Series championship in 1980.

Owens managed the 1983 team, affectionately known as the Wheeze Kids, to the World Series, only to lose in five games to the Baltimore Orioles.

Owens was given the nickname "Pope" by Dick Allen, who thought he resembled Pope Paul VI. It would be hard to find a member of the Phillies family held in higher esteem than Paul Owens.

In addition to Paul Owens, a number of baseball players who spent time as members of the Philadelphia Phillies have recently died as well. They include pitchers **Ken Brett**, **Johnny Klippstein**, **Tug McGraw** and Whiz Kids infielder **Mike Goliat**.

It seems only fitting that these former players be included and remembered in *Phillies: Where Have You Gone?*

Where Have You Gone?

KEN
BRETT

This much-traveled southpaw set a modern record by pitching for the most clubs, 10, during his career. Mike Morgan went on to break that mark by playing for 12 teams.

Ken Brett won at least 10 games four times during his career. Brett had great stuff, but arm problems plagued him for most of his 14 years in the majors. He first came on the scene with the Boston Red Sox in 1967 when he became the youngest pitcher to play in the World Series.

After spending parts of four seasons with the Bosox, Brett played a season in Milwaukee before winning 13 games for the '73 Phillies. Known as an outstanding hitter, he set a record by hitting a home run in four consecutive starts that year. The brother of Hall of Fame member George Brett, Ken also won 13 games in 1974 with the Pirates and in 1977 with the Chicago White Sox and California Angels.

Brett was the winning pitcher in the 1974 All-Star Game and also served up the 700th career home run of Hank Aaron. He finished in Kansas City, where he and George were teammates with the Royals.

Following his baseball career, Brett made television commercials, was a color commentator for the Angels and Mariners and was

PHILADELPHIA PHILLIES

KEN
BRETT   PITCHER

#31 KEN BRETT • PITCHER

Phillies, Red Sox, Brewers, Pirates, Yankees,
White Sox, Angels, Twins , Dodgers, Royals

**Born: 9/18/1948 Brooklyn NY • Died: 11/18/2003 Spokane WA
Height: 5-11 • Weight: 195 lbs. • Bats left • Throws left
14 year Major League Career: 83-85
Phillies 1 year • Major League Debut: 1967**

part owner of the Spokane Chiefs hockey team and the Spokane Indians baseball team.

Ken Brett died in Spokane on November 18, 2003 after a long battle with brain cancer at age 55.

A statement issued by the Royals said that Ken Brett was "valued highly as a member of our teams and even more highly as a friend. Ken will always hold a special place in our hearts and our memories."

MIKE GOLIAT

Though never an everyday major league player, Mike Goliat saw plenty of action during the 1950 campaign with the Whiz Kids. He appeared in 145 games, batting .234 and with 13 round-trippers and 64 RBIs, both career highs. He started the 1950 campaign off right getting four hits in the season's first game.

Goliat got off to a sluggish start in 1951, hitting .225 and was sent to the minor leagues before being sold to the St. Louis Browns later that year. He appeared in five games for St. Louis in 1951 and three the following year.

He spent the rest of his career in the International League, copping MVP honors in 1956 with Toronto. He was a player-coach for that team during four first-place seasons. Goliat hit .294 with 28 homers and 102 RBIs in 1957.

After baseball, he ran a small trucking business in Cleveland before working for the Ford Motor Company.

Mike Goliat died of heart failure on January 14, 2004 at his home in Seven Hills, Ohio.

#9 MIKE GOLIAT • INFIELD
Phillies, Browns

Born: 11/5/25 Yatesboro PA • Died: 1/14/2004 Seven Hills OH
Height: 6-0 • Weight: 180 lbs. • Bats right • Throws right
4 year Major League Career • .225 avg. • 20 HR • 99 RBI
Phillies 3 years • Major League Debut: 1949

JOHNNY KLIPPSTEIN

J ohnny Klippstein enjoyed a long major league career, first as a starter with the Cubs and Reds and then in his later years as a reliever.

He was offered his first pro contract at the age of 16, when he attended a tryout in Appleton, Wisconsin. He won 10 games for the 1953 Chicago Cubs and then a career-high 12 contests for Cincinnati in 1956.

Klippstein pitched in two World Series, for the Dodgers in 1959 and later for the Minnesota Twins in 1965, against the Dodgers. He had a fine year with the Phillies in 1963, going 5-6 in 49 games out of the bullpen with a 1.93 ERA. He was 2-1 for Philadelphia in 1964 before being sent to the Twins. He ended his 18-year career in 1967 with the Detroit Tigers.

During his career, he spent his off seasons as a mail carrier. Baseball's official historian, Jerome Holtzman, referred to Johnny Klippstein as "one of the most liked ballplayers of his time."

A staunch Cubs fan, Klippstein lived in Chicago for almost 50 years and was a Cubs season ticket holder. He died of prostate cancer on October 10, 2003, while listening to a Cubs defeat the Florida Marlins in a playoff game, 5-4. According to his son, Klippstein died shortly after the Cubs scored their fifth run.

#45 JOHNNY KLIPPSTEIN • PITCHER

Phillies, Cubs, Reds, Dodgers,
Indians, Senators, Twins, Tigers

Born: 10/17/1927 Washington DC • Died: 10/10/2003 Chicago IL
Height: 6-1 • Weight: 185 lbs. • Bats right • Throws right
18 year Major League Career: 101-118
Phillies 2 years • Major League Debut: 1950

TUG McGRAW

Y̶ou gotta believe!

That's what Tug McGraw said of the Miracle Mets of 1969 and the Phillies' lone world championship team in 1980. Unfortunately that phrase didn't help McGraw in his gallant battle against brain cancer, which he lost on January 5, 2004.

McGraw had been at spring training with the Phillies in March 2003, working with some young pitchers, when it was discovered that he had a tumor. Given just three weeks to live at the time, Tug underwent surgery and twice-a-day cancer treatments. With his joy for life and intensity that made him a successful athlete, he was able to live nearly a year after being diagnosed.

After a 4-16 beginning to his big-league career as a starter for the New York Mets, Frank Edwin "Tug" McGraw became one of the best closers in the game as his 180 career saves attest. Following 10 successful years with the Mets, Tugger was dealt to the Phillies in 1975 in a big trade that saw the Mets acquire catcher John Stearns in exchange.

"Tug was one of my favorite guys I ever spent time with," said his former teammate Gene Garber. "He was a lot more squared away

PHILADELPHIA PHILLIES

TUG
McGRAW

PITCHER

#45 TUG McGRAW • PITCHER

Phillies, Mets

Born: 8/30/1944 Martinez CA • Died: 1/5/2004 Nashville TN
Height: 6-0 • Weight: 185 lbs. • Bats right • Throws left
19 year Major League Career: 96-92
Phillies 10 years • Major League Debut: 1965

than people gave him credit for. He had created this image as a screwball and he had to live up to the image.

"I don't know of one teammate that didn't like Tug. He was always in a good mood and had lots of confidence. Of course, he also had doubts like the rest of us. But what a great guy."

McGraw took Philadelphia by storm as he became a popular personality. His strikeout of Kansas City's Willie Wilson in the bottom of the ninth inning in the sixth game of the 1980 World Series gave the Phillies their only World Series championship and forever etched Tug McGraw's leap of joy into the minds and hearts of an entire region.

"He was a wonderful friend," said former teammate Larry Christenson. "Tug told me that I was his best friend. He was always so friendly, bouncy and fun. Even if he felt down or upset, he kept it inside. He had such a big heart. My locker was between his and Steve Carlton's. Tug would walk into the locker room on a day he knew I was pitching and say loud enough for everyone to hear, 'Hey L.C., are you pitching tonight?' I'd say yes and then he would say, 'Then so am I.'

"He was so good to people, always friendly. He was crazy, but a good and charitable person. He was a pitcher who loved competing. He loved to fool the hitters. He was very good. It was all about trickery.

"I spoke with Tug two days before he died. We had the chance to say our good-byes."

Following his career, the father of country music star Tim McGraw became a sportscaster and writer in the area.

At one point during his fight against cancer, McGraw made personal appearances in the area again. But when he made his final stop at the final game at Veterans Stadium on September 28, it was obvious that Tugger was once again not well.

Still, his final year was quite an accomplishment for this lovable screw balling screwball who was given just three weeks to live. Sadly, Tug lost his battle with cancer in Nashville, surrounded by his family.

Celebrate the Heroes of Philadelphia Sports
in These Other Releases from Sports Publishing!